C000213649

Me and Mamie O'Rourke

A play

Mary Agnes Donoghue

Samuel French — London
New York - Toronto - Hollywood

© 1995 by Mary Agnes Donoghue

Rights of Performance by Amateurs are controlled by Samuel French Ltd, 52 Fitzroy Street, London W1P 6JR, and they, or their authorized agents, issue licences to amateurs on payment of a fee. **It is an infringement of the Copyright to give any performance or public reading of the play before the fee has been paid and the licence issued.**

The Royalty Fee indicated below is subject to contract and subject to variation at the sole discretion of Samuel French Ltd.

Basic fee for each and every
performance by amateurs   Code M
in the British Isles

The Professional Rights in this play are controlled by International Creative Management Inc, 40 West 57th Street, New York, NY 10019 USA.

The publication of this play does not imply that it is necessarily available for performance by amateurs or professionals, either in the British Isles or Overseas. Amateurs and professionals considering a production are strongly advised in their own interests to apply to the appropriate agents for consent before starting rehearsals or booking a theatre or hall.

ISBN 0 573 01844 8

Please see page iv for further copyright information

ME AND MAMIE O'ROURKE

First performed at the Palace Theatre, Watford, on 31st
January 1992, with the following cast:

Louise	Diana Hardcastle
Clark	Jeff Harding
David	Ron Berglas
Bibi	Patti Love

Directed by Robert Chetwyn
Designed by Alexandra Byrne

Subsequently performed at the Strand Theatre, London,
on 15th December 1993, with the following cast:

Louise	Jennifer Saunders
Clark	Benedick Blythe
David	Sean Chapman
Bibi	Dawn French

Directed by Robert Allan Ackerman
Designed by Ultz

COPYRIGHT INFORMATION

(See also page ii)

This play is fully protected under the Copyright Laws of the British Commonwealth of Nations, the United States of America and all countries of the Berne and Universal Copyright Conventions.

All rights including Stage, Motion Picture, Radio, Television, Public Reading, and Translation into Foreign Languages, are strictly reserved.

No part of this publication may lawfully be reproduced in ANY form or by any means — photocopying, typescript, recording (including video-recording), manuscript, electronic, mechanical, or otherwise—or be transmitted or stored in a retrieval system, without prior permission.

Licences for amateur performances are issued subject to the understanding that it shall be made clear in all advertising matter that the audience will witness an amateur performance; that the names of the authors of the plays shall be included on all programmes; and that the integrity of the authors' work will be preserved.

The Royalty Fee is subject to contract and subject to variation at the sole discretion of Samuel French Ltd.

In Theatres or Halls seating Four Hundred or more the fee will be subject to negotiation.

In Territories Overseas the fee quoted above may not apply. A fee will be quoted on application to our local authorized agent, or if there is no such agent, on application to Samuel French Ltd, London.

VIDEO-RECORDING OF AMATEUR PRODUCTIONS

Please note that the copyright laws governing video-recording are extremely complex and that it should not be assumed that any play may be video-recorded for whatever purpose without first obtaining the permission of the appropriate agents. The fact that a play is published by Samuel French Ltd does not indicate that video rights are available or that Samuel French Ltd controls such rights.

CHARACTERS

Louise
Clark
David
Bibi

The action takes place in the laundry-room in the basement of David's and Louise's house, which is built into a hillside in Los Angeles

Time — the present

THE SET

The large laundry-room looks like a one-room apartment —
containing, in addition to the washer and dryer, a stove,
refrigerator, deep utility sink, table and table lamp, several
hardback chairs, a small bed-turned-couch, shelves holding
books, a record-player and records, portable radio, wall
telephone, battered easy chair and reading lamp, dressmaker's dummy, sewing table and machine. Draped over the
dressmaker's dummy is a paper vest, carefully cut-out in the
shape of a hacking jacket. Mixed in with all this is the usual
collection of gardening equipment and cleaning equipment,
ironing board, boxes of old clothes and abandoned furniture
found stored in any ordinary basement. The wood walls are
unfinished and laced with fuse boxes, gas meters and exposed
water pipes. A light bulb hangs by a wire from the ceiling and
is partially covered by a cloth shade.

At the rear of the laundry-room to the far L is a flight of stairs
leading to the upper part of the house, which is above stage
and not visible. Behind the stairs is a darkened doorway
leading to another part of the basement. The stairs are covered
with a fine layer of plaster dust.

At the rear of the laundry-room to the far R is a door leading
out into a lush flower garden, which extends across the back
of the stage, past a row of windows set in the rear wall of the
room, and slopes into a hill which vanishes L. The flower
garden also extends a few feet around the R side of the
laundry-room, then runs in a narrow strip along the front of
the stage and ends in a small flight of winding wooden steps
that lead off the stage, as if the steps are winding up the
hillside and out of sight.

The personal touches in the room are attractive and distinc-
tive. The flowered slipcover on the easy chair is faded and
subtle, the vase on the table delicate and rare, the few bits of
furniture are well-polished antiques. It appears that a person
of sensitivity and taste has been driven by some unknown
force to set up house in the dark reaches of the cellar.

The following song lyrics are quoted by permission:

"Come Fly with Me" © Cahn Music Co. and Maraville Music Corp., U.S.A., Warner Chappell Music Ltd, London W1Y 3FA and The International Music Network Ltd, Buckhurst Hill, IG9 5NS. Reproduced by permission of International Music Publications Ltd

"If I had a Hammer (The Hammer Song)" Words and music by Lee Hays and Pete Seeger. TRO © Copyright 1958 (renewed) and 1962 (renewed). Ludlow Music Inc., New York, N.Y. Assigned to TRO Essex Music Ltd, London SW10 0SZ. Used by permission

"Three Little Fishies" by Saxie Dowell. Copyright © 1939 by Santly-Joy-Select Inc U.S.A.. Rights assigned to Joy Music Inc, U.S.A.. Campbell Connelly & Co. Ltd, 8-9 Frith Street, London W1V 5TZ. Used by permission. All rights reserved

"I'll Never Smile Again" by Ruth Lowe. © 1939 Pickwick Music Corp., assigned to MCA Music Publishing

A licence issued by Samuel French Ltd to perform this play does not include permission to use the Incidental music specified in this copy. Where the place of performance is already licensed by the PERFORMING RIGHT SOCIETY a return of the music used must be made to them. If the place of performance is not so licensed then application should be made to the Performing Right Society, 29 Berners Street, London W1.

A separate and additional licence from PHONOGRAPHIC PERFORMANCES LTD, Ganton House, Ganton Street, London W1 is needed whenever commercial recordings are used.

For Mary Becker
and
In Memory of
Robert Becker

ACT I

SCENE 1

The laundry-room. Saturday morning

The washer and drier are pounding away and an electric kettle is going. There is no-one in the room

Louise (*off*) Goodbye, have a wonderful time and don't forget to give Gloyd the banana bread ...

Louise enters, backing past the rear windows and waving goodbye. She is in her mid-thirties and wears her favourite old cotton dress, her favourite wool sweater and a pair of rubber boots. She pauses at the door

... and remember to help Grandma with the dishes and be kind to the dog, he's half-blind now, and don't make little jokes about Grandpa when he's in the room! Just because he can't speak doesn't mean he can't hear!

As she drops her hand, the washer suddenly lets out a terrible grinding sound and begins to rock violently, a piercing whistle comes from the electric kettle and an alarm clock goes off. Louise races to the kettle and turns it off, runs to the washer and gives it a vicious kick which stops the rocking and noise

(*Snatching up the clock and turning off the alarm; shouting*) Shake the lead out, rise and shine!

She quickly goes to the refrigerator, rips out the milk, eggs and bread, and pours the milk over a waiting bowl of cornflakes. She drops the bread into the toaster, then smashes the eggs into a bowl, mixing in pieces of shell, and starts beating them with one hand while pouring the water through a coffee filter with the other, her mind a million miles away. As the toast pops up, she ignores it, wandering toward the easy chair, lost in her own thoughts

Clark (*off*)   Shy one, shy one, shy one of my heart ...
                   She carries the dishes and lays them in a row,
                   To an isle in the water, with her would I go.

At the sound of Clark's voice Louise begins to smile with pleasure

   *Clark enters out of the gloom from the doorway under the stairs. He is
   immaculately dressed in very stylish casual clothes*

*Louise sinks into the chair, gazing in his direction with glazed eyes, a
dreamy expression on her face, the bowl forgotten in her hand*

Good-morning, darling. God, you look beautiful today, not that you
don't look beautiful every day, but today your beauty is positively
incandescent. Is that my breakfast you're cooking, dearest? I can't bear
it. I can't bear it that someone like you, beautiful, talented, possessed
of exceptional sensitivity and imagination thinks only of me, never of
herself, but how could it be different? You aren't simply Louise ... you
are Woman. Oh, but let me do something to make you happy, my little
blossom. Forget all this drudgery! Let's fly to Aspen for the weekend,
or better yet New York, our favourite suite at the Plaza, our table at Le
Circque ... No! I've got it! Let me take you on a shopping spree! You
know that's what I live for, don't you, my perfect angel? I live to make
you happy.

*David, a man Louise's age dressed in jeans, T-shirt and workboots,
enters and comes down the stairs*

*The washer starts rocking again, giving off the same grinding noise.
Louise is oblivious to it, staring at Clark with glazed eyes. David stares
at Louise as he walks to the washer, then suddenly gives it a violent kick,
bringing the grinding to an end*

David   What are you doing? A sensory deprivation exercise?

Louise spins around to him, noticing him for the first time

   Clark exits, disappearing back into the gloom

Louise   (*with sad longing*) No. Just thinking.

*David walks over to her, takes the bowl from her hands, lifts the goo
which is thick with shells, then walks to the counter and stirs the soggy
cornflakes*

David Is this my breakfast?

She nods. He dumps it all into the trash, takes the toast from the toaster and walks to the table

Louise I can make it again.
David Don't say things like that, Louise. I'm easily frightened.

He sits down and starts eating the toast. She goes to the drier and starts pulling clothes out and folding them. He watches her. She catches him watching her

Louise (*uneasily*) Why are you looking at me?
David You're in my line of vision.

She stares at him, then goes back to folding laundry. He watches her. She suddenly moves. His eyes follow

Louise I moved and you looked! What are you up to? What do you want?
David Are the boys gone?
Louise Aunt Vesta just picked them up.
David She's keeping them all weekend?
Louise Until Monday. What's this all about? Why are you asking questions, why are you looking at me, why are you out of bed before noon?
David Let's play a game.
Louise (*startled*) A game? What kind of a game?
David A guessing game and I go first. Why do you think I wanted a wake-up call this morning?
Louise (*cautiously*) I don't know.
David I know you don't know. The point is to guess.
Louise The luminous quality of the morning light makes your heart soar like a hawk.
David No.
Louise You're sick of sleeping fifteen hours a day?
David Wrong again.
Louise It made you feel employed.
David (*impatiently*) You're not even trying, Louise. Use your imagination. Obviously, I want to do something today. Guess what it is.
Louise Hang out at the news-stand.
David No.
Louise (*with hopeful excitement*) Meet with the accountant about paying our back taxes?

David No.

Louise No, of course not, that would be ridiculous.

David I'll give you a hint. What do I do when I'm on fire with new ideas, driven mad with creative excitement and desperate to express my individuality?

Louise (*staring at him; softly, scared*) You work at home.

David Yes!

Louise You're going to work at home?

David Yes!

Louise (*anxiously*) On what?

David Guess!

Louise (*with a nervous smile*) Well. There's so much to choose from, I don't know where to start ... (*Hopefully*) You're going to tie up the exhaust pipe on the truck?

David Cold.

Louise You're going to repair the back porch steps?

David Cold.

Louise (*with sudden excitement*) I know! You're finally going to put the roof back on!

David Icy cold.

Louise But there's nothing else that would appeal to you ... (*Pause. With quiet dread*) Unless you're going to work inside the house.

David Getting warm.

Louise You're going to work upstairs ...?

David Getting warmer!

Louise You're going to work in a bedroom?

David Getting hot!

Louise You're going to work in the boys' bedroom?

David Getting boiling hot!

Louise You're going to do something to the walls in the boys' bedroom?

David *Sizzling hot*!

Louise (*with a wail of despair*) You're going to tear down the walls in the boys' bedroom!

David Yes!

Louise No! Please! You have to stop! Those are the only interior walls we have left!

David My point exactly, and that's why I cannot stop! They must come down today!

Louise But where will our children sleep?

David Where they have always slept, on beds, not walls.

Louise (*staring at him, a towel clutched in her arms*) Why? When there is so much to rebuild in this house, why must you always tear things down?

David Why? You know why. Rebuilding costs money and we don't have any. And do you know why we don't have any money?

Louise No. I've often wondered but it never got me anywhere.

David We don't have any money because in this world genius is not rewarded, it's punished and because it is punished I am out of work.

Louise Oh, David, I know you're a wonderful architect, there's no doubt about ——

David Wonderful! I'm not wonderful! People who design shopping malls are wonderful. I wouldn't spit on a shopping mall. I'm not wonderful, I'm revolutionary, visionary, unique!

Louise Yes, I know all that, but still, I don't think people want to live in pods.

David Who cares what people want! I'm an artist, not a social worker.

Louise But they have to live in what you build and when it all comes out in the wash ... (*she glances at the towel and folds it*) they don't want to do it in the laundry pod which is fifty yards from the storage pod, especially in the rain!

David My imagination is an independent force, Louise, not a servant to convention.

Louise But David, don't you understand? People need walls and staircases and hallways. How can you hang a picture without a wall, how can you make an entrance at a party without a staircase, how can you loiter in the hall without a hallway? And doors, David, doors! How can you tell a secret without a door to shut behind you, how can you eavesdrop without a keyhole? David. How can you build pods?

David To defy people like you. You have a middle-class streak that has always chilled me. (*He walks to the staircase and pulls a sledgehammer out from under it*) When I am finished absolutely nothing in this pretentious little hillside tenement you bought behind my back ——

Louise It was my money! Uncle Honey was my uncle, not yours, and he left the money to me!

David Yeah, and you left me with the payments. (*Coldly*) Nothing in this structural atrocity, this aesthetic eyesore, this squalid monument to middle-class mediocrity will be left standing if it offends me and all of it offends me! I can live with rubble, I cannot live with green-flecked linoleum!

Louise Don't underestimate that stuff. It hides dirt so well you could kill a cow on this floor and not know it an hour later.

David (*tortured*) Why did you do it? Why did you sneak out and buy this depressing little service station ——

Louise Ranger station. It's a depressing little ranger station.

David And now it's a station of the cross and I'm the poor slob hauling the lumber. (*Fiercely*) In the warehouse, our lives had substance. Each day was a daring experiment in socialization.

Louise We were living like rats in a behavioural sink! If we'd stayed much longer we would have started biting each other over food!

David Don't be ridiculous. We were rarely threatened by a food shortage.

Louise We were living in a windowless, concrete box, with the bodies of dead pigeons on the skylights and our few sticks of furniture hanging from hooks! We were exhausted from standing up all the time!

David You could have unhooked the chairs.

Louise You hung them so high the children and I couldn't reach them! Do you have any idea what it feels like to want to sit down and not be able to reach the chairs?

David I don't care! The warehouse was mine! Every nail had a purpose and my life was a continuous creative discourse! This place ... this place is an outrage and nothing in it will escape my wrath. (*Grimly, threatening*) By the end of this weekend, nothing will be left standing except the shell. Absolutely nothing.

Louise (*with a resigned sigh*) Oh, well. Except for a stray wall here and there and this cellar I guess that's all that's standing now. Just don't demolish any retaining walls without warning me. The last time you did that we lost the last of the dining-room furniture and the cat. The boys were inconsolable.

David (*softly, puzzled*) I never understood their attachment to that furniture ... (*Suddenly. Hard*) One more thing, Louise. I will be finished in the boys' room by Sunday. Do you know what that means?

Louise No, I don't, and I don't want to.

David It means that when I'm finished in the boys' room there will only be one thing left to eliminate.

She stares at him

Louise (*softly, lethally*) You wouldn't dare touch that!

David Why not?

Louise (*quickly walking over to him; outraged*) Because it's mine!

David It's not yours, it's ours and I can't stand the sight of it!

Louise But we had an agreement!

David (*looking back at her*) What agreement?

Louise That you'd leave it alone.

David I never agreed to that. I simply agreed to leave it until the end and Sunday will be the end.

They stare at each other

Get used to the idea, Louise. I'm going to do it.

He exits overhead

Louise stands staring up the stairs after him

A pretty woman in her early thirties, dressed in a very chic 1930s suit and hat and carrying two suitcases, comes bounding down the hillside steps. This is Bibi. She walks across the front of the stage to the laundry-room door

Bibi (*singing*)   I'll never smile again
                              Until I smile at you
                              I'll never laugh again
                              Until I laugh ... at you ...
(*She mutters*) That can't be right.

At that moment there is a terrible ripping sound above the laundry-room, then a tremendous crash. Just as Bibi walks through the door, rubble comes tumbling down the stairs and a wave of plaster dust filters down over the room from above. Both women ignore it as if it is something that happens all the time

(*Thrilled*) Louise!

As Louise spins around, Bibi poses dramatically in the doorway. Louise's face lights up with delight

Louise Oh, Bibi! Where did you get that suit?

During the rest of this scene, there is the faint sound of hammering overhead and an occasional small crash. The women ignore it. Bibi walks in and drops her suitcases near the table

Bibi I got it for a song from the estate of an old movie star who blew her brains out in a Bob's Big Boy. (*Amazed*) Do you believe it? Every stain came out! (*She dances around the room*) Oh, Louise, I feel as if I could just dance the night away in a suit like this, as if I could drown in champagne, as if ... (*she stumbles over the rubble*) What's this? The walls in the boys' room?
Louise Yes. He finally got them.
Bibi (*picking up a cloth and wiping plaster dust off surfaces*) Oh, well, it's not as bad as when he took the roof off the living-room. All those

mice. (*Delighted*) I don't think I've ever seen a more dramatic display of fright and flight response! (*With a sudden sad sigh*) It's funny though. As difficult as all this has been, it makes me a little sad to think it's finally coming to an end. It feels like the end of an era. (*She sings nostalgically*)

> If I had a hammer,
> I'd hammer in the morning,
> I'd hammer in the evening,
> All over this land ...

(*She gives Louise a melancholy smile*) And now, his hammer is still.

Louise (*grimly*) Not necessarily.

Bibi (*dismissively*) Oh, don't be silly, Louise. He wouldn't dare touch that.

Louise He's threatening to.

Bibi Well, of course he is. Give the guy a break. That's how he has his fun, isn't it?

Louise (*uneasily*) Yes ... but there was nothing playful about this threat. It was delivered with a chilling intensity, as if this final act of defiance against the decorative arts had become an obsession with him ... (*Panicky*) I'm frightened. I've watched him over the months, slowly working his way toward it, hammering, tearing, ripping, knocking ... his eye always on it, hungry and cold. It's the only thing in this house I ever asked him not to touch! (*Frantically*) He's going for it, Bibi, he's finally going for it and I don't know why!

Bibi (*staring at her; scared*) It sounds to me as if he's trying to force you to take a stand!

Louise No!

Bibi Yes! Why else this sudden change in tactics? (*Softly*) Thank God I read military history. (*To Louise*) Pay attention, Louise. If you take a stand and he wins, it could lead to total domination! He must be stopped!

Louise But how?

Bibi looks at her thoughtfully as she dusts a table top

Bibi (*suddenly*) Felix!

Louise Felix ...?

Bibi Yes, your very old Uncle Felix with the diminished mental capacity and extremely unattractive personal hygiene habits. From what you said the other day, it doesn't sound as if he's going to make it through the weekend.

Louise What does that have to do with anything ...?

Bibi Money! If David had the money to build pods he might lose interest in this final act of destruction.

Louise (*aghast*) Are you suggesting I use the death of another human being to promote my own self-interest?

Bibi Yes.

Louise (*firmly*) Well, even if I wanted to, I can't. That money is for the boys' college fund.

Bibi They're still in playschool.

Louise Felix tends to rally.

Bibi He's ninety-two and enough is enough. When exactly is the ——

Louise Don't say deadline! (*Horrified*) And how could you say enough is enough about a person's existence!

Bibi (*dusting again*) Because life is not a condo, Louise, it is a rental unit and Felix has overstayed his lease.

Louise (*staring at her, then finally picking up her broom*) We are both going to forget we ever had this conversation and before I go to sleep tonight I'm going to pray for Felix's health. (*She sweeps*) Put that cloth down, Bibi. You'll get your suit dirty.

Bibi I told you it cleans like a dream. Expensive fabric always does. And speaking of that, one of those suitcases is full of dirty laundry. May I?

Louise Sure, but I'm ——

Bibi (*staring out the window with excitement*) Louise! Quick! Look!

Louise rushes to the window, clutching the broom

Louise (*alarmed*) What?

Bibi What do you see?

Louise (*searching*) A dog walking past the carob trees and a cat eating grass near the tomato plants.

Bibi No. You see a cat displaying embarrassment as he makes a territorial deferment to larger and more powerful aggressor.

Louise I see you've been hard at work.

Bibi (*with a weary sigh*) What choice do I have? Animal behaviourism is a demanding discipline. Still, it gives back more than it takes. I spent a good part of yesterday doing field work ...

Louise Where?

Bibi The zoo. Captives make quite a study! First of all, they can't get away, and secondly it is the only environment where the observed are also the observers. I think there's a lot to be learned there, the pros aren't doing anything about it so I just thought, amateur or not, I might just make it my area of expertise. I mean, think about it. We know what we make of them, but what do they make of us? Dizzying, isn't it?

(*Excitedly*) I knocked off a letter to Jane Goodall about it first thing this morning and I just think I might finally get her attention.

Louise (*knowingly*) No-one's so famous they can afford to turn their nose up at an original idea. (*She goes back to sweeping*) I'm doing whites next.

Bibi (*dusting*) Mine are coloureds, but I can wait. (*Embarrassed, nervously*) He's not picking me up until this afternoon.

Louise (*quickly spinning around with excitement*) It's definite?

Bibi (*uncertain, nervously*) Well, it could be definite.

Louise What are you talking about? Of course it's definite. Why are you dressed like that? To go to the corner store for a pack of cigarettes?

Bibi Well, I can't help having my doubts. I only met him for twenty minutes at a check-out counter two months ago.

Louise Some things are instant.

Bibi I only heard from him yesterday.

Louise He lost your phone number.

Bibi Why didn't he look it up?

Louise He couldn't remember your last name.

Bibi How did he find me now?

Louise He found your phone number.

Bibi I only talked to him once.

Louise You only have to talk once to plan a trip.

Bibi He has a girlfriend.

Louise She moved out.

Bibi Yesterday.

Louise So what?

Bibi She might come back.

Louise Who says?

Bibi It's happened before.

Louise It doesn't mean it'll happen again.

Bibi I asked him to pick me up here.

Louise Why?

Bibi I wanted you to see his face in case you have to contact the police.

Louise Oh, for God's sake, Bibi, what has happened to your sense of romance and adventure?

Bibi (*embarrassed*) Well, actually, I was so excited about this trip I couldn't sleep last night. (*Excitedly*) I spent hours talking to myself in front of the mirror.

Louise That's the spirit! About what?

Bibi Oh, the usual things people talk about ... childhood memories, do crystals heal, the pros and cons of a strong central government, the ozone layer. You cannot be casual about falling in love.

Louise Absolutely not. It's an art and all art requires practise.

Bibi Nothing can be left to chance, certainly not conversation. It would be an act of criminal negligence to allow a badly timed remark, an awkward turn of the head or a crooked smile seen from the wrong angle to destroy the tender stirrings of a great, perhaps — I'm almost afraid to say it — an even legendary, romance.

Louise Oh, Bibi! Are you saying what I think you're saying?

Bibi (*with breathless excitement*) Yes, Louise, I am! I know it seems precipitous, but I can't help feeling that this time, if he actually shows up, it's going to be the real thing! I think he's the one I've been waiting for all my life and this breathless happiness I feel is the beginning of something big, a great and consuming passion and I won't let anything nip it in the vine!

Louise In the bud. Things die on the vine. It takes longer. (*She suddenly walks to the dressmaker's dummy, pulls the paper vest from it and holds it up for Bibi to see*) Speaking of death, what do you think of this?

Bibi (*gasping with delight*) It's brilliant!

Louise (*flattered*) Do you think so ...?

Bibi That is, without question, the most fabulous design for a bullet-proof vest I've ever seen! Not that I've ever seen any, of course, but still (*she takes the vest and slips it on over her suit, modelling it*) ... this is divine! You are going to clean up with these, Louise. The world is just crawling with walking targets who would pay an arm and a leg for eye-catching protection to wear to opening night galas, inaugurations, theme parks ... You're a genius!

Louise (*with a flattered laugh*) Oh, no.

Bibi (*taking off the vest and replacing it on the dummy*) You are!

Louise (*with another flattered laugh*) No ... do you really think so ...?

Bibi Absolutely.

Louise (*smiling modestly*) Well ... over the years people have said I have a unique creative vision.

Bibi You just haven't had a chance to pursue it, that's all.

Louise It's true ... I have so many incredible design ideas ...

Bibi Let's not forget the slipcovers in a dog-hair pattern! Every housewife's dream!

Louise Exactly, but every time I try to do something of my own, someone gets in the way ... the children ... David ... (*Suddenly, tensely*) Clark.

Bibi (*amazed*) Clark ...? You've heard from Clark ...?

Louise (*tortured*) No, I haven't heard from him, I just can't get him out of my mind! He's all I think about! I'm obsessed!

Clark appears in his doorway, dressed for polo

Clark Hurry into the garden, darling. The new polo pony just arrived.

Bibi What brought this on?

Louise I don't know.

Clark I do. (*He sings the first two lines of "The Way We Were"*)

Bibi Memories, probably, of the days you left behind.

Louise There are so many ... the simplest things made us happy ...

Clark I thought after the opera we'd dismiss the servants and dine alone.

Louise And I relied on his uncompromising honesty for self-knowledge. When Clark said something about me, I knew it was true.

Clark Be sure to wear the black, Louise. It shows off your lovely shoulders to perfection.

Bibi Even if Clark was your ticket to paradise, Louise, that train left without you ten years ago.

Clark There is always the return trip.

Louise He was so handsome, so young ... Oh, and his seat was extraordinary. Everyone commented on it.

Bibi (*startled*) I think that's rude.

Louise I meant on a horse. (*Passionately*) His love for me consumed him, Bibi, he lived for me! (*Tragically*) I wonder if he ever recovered from that loss. When I left him for David he was destroyed. I just hope that when I broke his heart I didn't destroy his brilliant future in medicine as well. He had such promise, so much to give! I almost called him last night!

Clark (*holding an imaginary telephone receiver*) Louise! My darling, Louise, at last!

Bibi Why didn't you do it?

Clark (*into the imaginary phone*) Louise who? No, I'm sorry. That name doesn't ring a bell.

Louise He's married, he has children ... one word from me could destroy it all.

Bibi (*with envious longing*) After all this time?

Louise (*with a melancholy smile*) I don't know what it is about me ... men just can't seem to get over me. (*Suddenly, tensely*) Do you know what I keep thinking, Bibi?

The hammering overhead has stopped, but they are so caught up in conversation they do not notice

Bibi No.

Clark I do.

Louise I keep thinking that maybe I did it all wrong. Maybe I made a terrible mistake ten years ago. Instead of doing what I did maybe I should have ——

There is a sound overhead and they instinctively turn toward the stairs

David appears on the stairs. He looks at them suspiciously. Clark exits, disappearing back into the darkness under the stairs

Bibi and Louise go back to cleaning

Bibi (*cheerily*) David! How are the walls going?
David They're gone. (*He comes down the stairs*) What were you two talking about just now?
Bibi (*cheerily*) Oh, nothing. Just the usual.
David Then why were you whispering?
Louise We weren't whispering.
David Why did you stop talking when you saw me?
Bibi To say hallo.
David Why haven't you started talking again?
Louise We are. We're talking to you.

He looks at them suspiciously again as he walks past them toward the door, then he stops when he spots Bibi's suitcases

David You're going away?
Bibi Yes. In a couple of hours.
David (*surprised*) You took the job in New York?
Bibi Oh, God, no, I couldn't do that! It's so far away and I wouldn't just be a cook in a restaurant like that, I'd be a chef. They'd want me to sign a contract, stay for a few years, and I have to be ready to move at a moment's notice.
David Of course. Your commitment to science. You know what I like best about you, Bibi?
Bibi My recipe for chicken and dumplings and my exquisite taste in shoes.
David Your originality. You're the only uneducated, aspiring scientist I've ever met. Most people with your lack of qualifications are actresses.
Bibi Say what you like, animal behaviourism is a new field and there's still room for raw talent to succeed. I just need to meet the right people. What do think got Jane Goodall where she is today? Her credentials?
Louise Her contacts!
Bibi Exactly.
David Where are you off to then? Brazil, to study the minor leaf monkey?
Bibi No. Until the right expedition comes along, I'm settling for a week in Rosarita Beach.

David Well, I'm settling for the news-stand. (*He walks to the door*)
Remember, Louise. Sunday night. (*He walks out*)
Bibi (*wistfully*) He's so handsome when he's scaring us.

He exits R, passing the row of windows

*The two women smile and wave, then the second he vanishes they quickly
turn to each other*

Bibi So?
Louise So I think I took a wrong turn in my life, Bibi!
Bibi What wrong turn? What do you mean?
Louise I mean I never should have ——

David reappears suddenly in the window and they fall silent

David God, you two are fast, but one of these days I know I'll catch you.

He exits R

Louise — married David!
Bibi (*lowering her dusting cloth in shock*) No, Louise, I know times have
been hard, but you've gone too far now!
Louise I know! Ten years too far!

*Clark appears in the doorway, wearing a smoking-jacket and drinking
a martini*

Clark You haven't gone far enough ... (*He sings*)
        Come fly with me,
        Let's float down to Peru ...
Bibi Good marriages don't just happen, Louise, you have to work at them
and work requires discipline. I admit that discipline can be painful at
times, but without it we are nothing! Oh Louise!
Clark (*singing*) In llama land there's a one-man band
        Who'll toot his flute for you ...
Bibi Don't you see? All accomplishment depends on discipline and
being David's wife isn't just an emotional commitment, it's ... well ...
(*as a revelation*) it's a gruelling form of discipline! You're not just
married, Louise! You're in training!
Louise (*savagely*) For what? Survival in a prison camp? I've had it! I
don't think I can take much more of this, Bibi!

Bibi (*sombrely*) Oh, but Louise, you'll hate it out here. It's a swamp for a woman without a man. Take it from a long-time swamp-dweller. The loneliness, the despair. After a while, you find yourself developing deep emotional ties to things that aren't even mammals! (*Soothingly*) You're having a little crack-up, that's all. You've been under a lot of strain for a while ...

Louise A while? For three, long, rubble-filled years!

Bibi Well, I know, I've lived through it too ... not that you can blame me for being here all the time when you consider the squalid conditions in that hillside hacienda I rent a room in ... (*Outraged*) Do you know what that filthy landlord of mine has started doing with his mosaics?

Louise I'm not interested in your landlord's obsession with mosaics right now!

Bibi He has taken to entombing his dead pets in the walls of the garage!

Louise Bibi! Pay attention! My family does not divorce!

Louise I know. I've always thought it was such a charming trait.

Louise I can't leave him and I can't stay. What am I going to do?

Clark (*singing, fading back into the gloom*)
> Where it's perfect for a flying honeymoon they say,
> Come fly with me, let's fly, let's fly away ...

He exits

Bibi You have one of two choices. You could kill David, which I don't recommend, or you could do nothing.

Louise I have to do something!

Bibi No, you don't. More sudden changes in tactics could prove disastrous.

Louise Disastrous how?

Bibi Impossible to predict. You have only once choice. You will have to wait.

Louise Wait for what?!

Bibi For Felix! (*Passionately*) He's the answer to all your problems, Louise. If David was busy building pods you might not want to leave him.

Louise (*softly, amazed*) Do you really think so ...? (*Puzzled*) I can't imagine not wanting to leave David ...

Bibi (*excitedly*) With David off your back, you'll finally be free! Think of it, Louise! Free to pursue your destiny! Free to show the world who you really are! Free, Louise, to finally do the unspeakable!

Louise (*softly, fascinated*) The unspeakable? What's that?

Bibi What's that? Look around you, Louise. Isn't it obvious? You'll finally be free ... (*triumphantly*) to rebuild!

Louise stares at her with dull wonder as if she has never heard the word before

Louise (*softly, dazed*) Rebuild?
Bibi (*inspiring*) Yes, Louise, rebuild! You will finally be able to explore the depths of your genius by rebuilding this house! With this as your goal, you cannot fail! (*Impassioned*) The darkest hour of your great struggle is approaching, Louise, so be strong of heart, fight the brave fight and just when you think defeat is upon you let that simple but stirring word repeat over and over in your head and you will triumph. Rebuild, Louise. Rebuild, rebuild, rebuild.
Louise (*horrified*) I've never waited for anyone to die before.
Bibi No, I haven't either. Partly because I don't think it's a nice thing to do, but mainly because I don't know any sick people with money. (*Firmly*) View it as a learning experience. Finding out just how callous and greedy you are can lead to growth.

They stare at each other

Bibi Rebuild, Louise. Rebuild, rebuild, rebuild.
Louise (*staring at her; softly, wondering*) Rebuild ... rebuild, rebuild ... (*With sudden excitement*) Rebuild!

Black-out

SCENE 2

Late Saturday night. The room is in darkness except for a spot c

Louise and Clark are in a tight embrace in front of the table. He is wearing a white doctor's coat and a stethoscope hangs from his neck. As they speak, a late Beethoven quartet plays softly in the background

Louise (*desperately*) But, my darling, if the treatment fails and the President dies what will they do to you?
Clark This is a third-world nation and he is a despot. I will be executed.
Louise (*desperately*) The risk is too great! Oh, but how can I ask you to turn away from this grave responsibility. You are a man of medicine!
Clark (*passionately*) My only fear is for you, Louise! If things go badly, you could be executed too!
Louise (*tearful but brave*) Don't worry about me! If the President dies the entire continent will explode into war. My safety means nothing when the safety of millions is at stake!

*He throws his arms around her and holds her tightly as the Lights begin
to come up*

*We now see that Bibi's open suitcases, spilling clothes, sit in front of the
washer, the music is coming from the record player, a bottle and two half-
full glasses of wine sit on the table, and a great stack of magazines sit on
the floor next to the easy chair*

   *Bibi enters, backing past the garden windows, clutching a fistful of
   herbs and gazing intently at something. Her hat is gone and she wears
   an apron over her suit*

Bibi Here kitty, kitty ... here kitty, kitty ...

*Clark suddenly releases Louise from his embrace and holds her at arm's
length, a tragic expression on his face*

Clark Remember, Louise. If I die, I will speak your name with my final
breath.

   He quickly turns, heads for the door under the stairs and exits

Louise (*as he goes; with a desperate cry*) Oh, my brave darling! Why did
we ever come to this terrible place on our Easter vacation?

The Lights have come up to full and Clark has vanished

Bibi (*backing into the room*) Here kitty, kitty ... a distress signal if I ever
saw one ... here little kitty ... didn't you hear me, puss ...? (*With an
exasperated shriek*) I said here kitty, kitty, you flea-infested, mangy
piece of ——

*At that moment, the telephone rings, cutting her off. Bibi and Louise turn
quickly to each other with tense expressions. Their eyes meet in a silent
message, they hesitate for one more ring, then both of them lunge for the
ringing phone at the same time. Louise reaches it first and snatches up
the receiver*

Louise (*hopefully*) Hallo? ... (*Snapping*) Yes, of course I love you, I'm
your mother, aren't I? ... Yes. ... I mean it. ... OK. Good-night.

She hangs up and they both take large gulps of wine

   I'm so ashamed!

Bibi (*filling the wine glasses; comfortingly*) You can't be a good mother all the time.

Louise I mean about Felix!

Bibi Oh. That. It's perfectly normal to feel ashamed when you're wishing someone dead. At least you don't know him well. Longing for the death of someone you know and like must be very unpleasant..

Louise (*tenderly*) I remember him as a strange, enigmatic man ... when I was a very small child he used to visit us at Christmas. He had a lovely moustache, like a walrus, and he always used to say, "You're talking through your hat."

Bibi (*puzzled*) What does that mean?

Louise We never knew. Over and over, all day long, no matter what anybody said to him all he would say back was, "You're talking through your hat."

Bibi He sounds like a jerk.

Louise He was.

Bibi Will you get bulletins?

Louise No. No bulletins for distant relatives. I'll just get one call. The decisive call.

Bibi (*glancing at the clock*) It doesn't look like I'm going to get any calls.

Louise He's only seven hours late. He might have a dead battery.

Bibi Unlike Felix.

The phone rings. Bibi looks at Louise, then puts her hands over her face

Bibi I can't answer it, I'm too anxious!

Louise hesitates, then snatches up the receiver

Louise Hallo? ... (*Pause. Sombrely*) Just a moment, please. (*She turns to Bibi and slowly holds out the receiver to her*) It's for you.

Bibi lowers her hands, looks into Louise's eyes, then squares her shoulders and takes the receiver

Bibi Hallo? (*Cheerfully*) Oh, hi! What a delightful surprise! ... What? ... No! Of course not! ... Are you serious? ... No! ... Wonderful! ... OK! ... Divine! ... Goodbye! (*She hangs up*)

Louise (*as Bibi hangs up*) The girlfriend's back.

Bibi For lunch.

Louise The trip's off?

Bibi Delayed.

Louise Until when?

Bibi Tomorrow morning.

Louise Long lunch.

Bibi I have to make a salad. (*She rushes to the refrigerator and while she speaks, she pulls a variety of vegetables out of it*) Happiness calls for a soufflé, tragedy requires a robust soup, but anxiety just screams for a salad. There is nothing more soothing to the restless heart than the clean, pure taste of the glistening lettuce leaf, the sweet tang of the humble carrot, the sharp but uncomplicated bite of the simple scallion ... (*Desperately*) Louise! I need to hear the plan again!

They both sit down at the table with their wine

Louise Any day now you will get a reply to all those letters you write to Jane Goodall and she'll invite you to join an expedition to Abyssinia where you will study the social habits of the grey baboon.

Bibi They have been shamefully ignored.

Louise Because you're not an academic you will look at things with an original eye.

Bibi And draw conclusions that will rock the scientific community.

Louise Your best-selling book will be turned into a documentary series on prime-time television, narrated by your new best friend David Attenborough, and you will earn enough money to not only buy a fast car and a cellular phone, you will also be able to finance more expeditions.

Bibi The Macoca monkey is just screaming for attention.

Louise And while you're studying the Macoca you will finally meet the man of your dreams.

Bibi A molecular biologist with a nice camera.

Louise And the two of you will spend your lives travelling to the far corners of the earth making love and scientific history.

Bibi sighs deeply with contentment and takes a large swig of wine. Louise takes a sip of hers and smiles softly

Louise Now you tell me.

Bibi You are going to design the first couturier bullet-proof vest, which Karl Lagerfeld will want to include in his spring collection.

Louise We will become close friends.

Bibi The resulting publicity, along with the proceeds from the sale of the vests to celebrities marked for extinction by terrorists, will provide you with the money and recognition to finally make fashion history! You, Louise, will design the first, truly chic, off-the-rack, paramilitary line! You will be the toast of every third-world country and will be invited to endless Hollywood parties.

Louise At first David will be consumed with jealousy over my staggering success and wealth.

Bibi Paralysed, but eventually, through your contacts in the entertainment industry, he will be asked to build several pod dwellings for highly influential people in Las Vegas. These pods will excite so much interest he will appear on the cover of every important architectural magazine and also be the recipient of endless cash prizes!

Louise In time, he might even be asked to build an entire pod city ... (*with intense desire*) far, far away ... in a distant land ...

Bibi (*inspiring*) So be strong, Louise, work hard, and be patient! Very few people are given the chance to dream great dreams, but you are definitely one of that select group so no matter how rough the road, how distant the destination, how impossible the dream, you must have the heart and strength of character never to lose sight of the goal! With courage, Louise, it will all be yours! All!

Louise Oh, Bibi!

Bibi What?

Louise I always have so much fun with you!

Bibi I know! It's amazing, isn't it? When you consider all the horrible things we've been through together. Remember when my ex-husband left me and took all my crêpe pans? I almost lost my job at Chez-Modest!

Louise And the trip to Wisconsin with the boys when the car kept breaking down and we ran out of money?

Bibi God that was grim! You broke your ankle falling off the bridge in that miniature golf course and I almost went blind driving the rest of the way myself.

Louise Oh, and the night on that smelly old stream! The mosquitoes!

Bibi The boys cried and cried ... (*Dreamily*) I saw my first goldfinch.

Louise I've never fought with anybody the way I fought with you on that trip.

Bibi Oh, I know. Remember when we lost first gear and you blamed me? I sat up all night in that dirty little diner writing vicious things about you in my diary.

Louise I called you a petty bitch. (*Warmly*) God that was a wonderful trip.

Pause as they sip their wine, fondly remembering their trip. Louise suddenly looks at Bibi and smiles slightly

Louise It's funny, isn't it?

Bibi What?

Louise That we always have so much fun together. I've never had as much fun with anybody.

Bibi Me neither.
Louise Not with David.
Bibi Not with any of my boyfriends and never with my husband.
Louise Not even with Clark ... of course, all-consuming passions that
   shake the very foundations of your being can't be considered fun.
Bibi Absolutely not.
Louise I've had the most fun with you.
Bibi And I with you. It is funny isn't it?
Louise Yes.

Pause. Bibi looks at her oddly

Bibi Very funny.
Louise What do you mean?

Pause

Bibi Louise, have you ever wondered ...?

Pause

Louise Wondered what?
Bibi Wondered if ... (*She pauses; then, rapidly*) Louise. Do you think we
   might be lesbians?

Louise looks at her, appalled

   *Clark appears in the doorway dressed in nothing but a leopardskin
   loincloth*

Clark Not my Louise! I can vouch for that!

*He lets out a large Tarzan yell, hitting his chest loudly with his fists,
then exits back into the darkness*

Louise If I was a lesbian, I'd know by now! I am an open, aware and
   sexually active person!
Bibi When was the last time you slept with David?
Louise (*defensively*) That has nothing to do with it! In all marriages of
   any duration there are always periods of ... restraint. (*In self-
   congratulatory tones*) My sexual relations with men have always been
   deeply satisfying. As a matter of fact, all of them said I was the best they
   ever had.

Bibi (*dismissively*) Everybody always says that.
Louise (*annoyed*) I don't believe you. (*Suddenly*) I think the only reason
you suggested what you just did is because you're having doubts about
your own sexuality!
Bibi Are you serious? My inability to resist male love is at the bottom of
all my problems in life!
Louise You could be overcompensating.
Bibi Well, whatever I'm doing, I'm not lusting after you, I can promise
you that!
Louise I'm relieved.

*Bibi starts making the salad and Louise picks up her scissors and a
magazine. She snips in silence for a moment*

I certainly don't want you either!

They continue with their tasks, not looking at each other

Bibi Good. If you did I'd be out that door.

Pause. Louise suddenly lowers her scissors and looks at Bibi

Louise Bibi?
Bibi (*working*) Yes?
Louise Do you think we want each other but we don't know it because
we're sexually repressed?
Bibi Well, it is a little weird, don't you think? Here we sit, year after year,
having fun! It's unnatural!
Louise It's true I always get a little thrill when I know you're coming
over. I wouldn't call it sexual exactly, but it is thrilling.
Bibi Sometimes after a rotten night in the restaurant when everything
I've cooked tastes like sawdust I think, "Well, at least I'll see Louise
later," and I feel happy.
Louise To take so much pleasure in each other's company just isn't right,
is it?
Bibi (*emphatically*) No, it certainly is not.

They sit down at the table and take large gulps of wine

Louise I've never said this before, but I've always thought you were
pretty.
Bibi I've always thought you were handsome.
Louise (*offended*) Handsome?

Bibi You know what I mean. A handsome woman, elegant, you have a
   timeless face.
Louise You have fabulous hair.
Bibi You have great legs.
Louise (*with vain pleasure*) I do, don't I?
Bibi Not that great. (*Suddenly*) I've never felt any desire to kiss you.
Louise I've never wanted to kiss you either.
Bibi I've never wanted you that way at all.
Louise Maybe it's because we're too afraid to even think about it.
Bibi Maybe.

There is a moment's silence, then Bibi leaps up and goes back to the salad

   Well, I'd better get on with this before everything wilts.

Pause. Louise watches her

Louise Bibi?
Bibi Yes?
Louise Maybe we should try it.
Bibi (*cautiously*) Try what?
Louise You know.

Bibi turns to look at her and they both break into nervous laughter

Bibi How?
Louise How should I know? But nothing too intense at first. It'll give us
   the creeps.

Bibi looks at Louise for a moment, then picks up her glass

Bibi OK, but we have to get drunker.

*They both down their glasses of wine, then Louise refills them. They stand
awkwardly, looking at one another*

Louise So! Where do we start?
Bibi Let's try holding hands.
Louise OK.

*They sit down, facing the audience, and hold each other's hand. A
moment passes*

   Your hand's sweating.

Bibi So's yours. It's not attractive.

Bibi takes her hand away and sips her wine. Louise takes a big slug from her glass. They put their glasses down

Bibi Maybe one of us should put her arm around the other one.
Louise A full embrace?
Bibi No, just an arm around the shoulders.
Louise Which one?
Bibi I don't know.
Louise You're more aggressive than I am. You do it.

Bibi shrugs, then puts her arm around Louise. They stare straight ahead for a moment

Bibi (*suddenly*) You're very mushy.
Louise The word is voluptuous and you don't exactly feel like a weight-lifter yourself. This is awkward. I'll put my head on your shoulder.
Bibi OK.

Louise puts her head on Bibi's shoulder. Pause

Louise Nice scent.
Bibi Thanks. So's yours. Is that the stuff they test on people instead of animals?
Louise Yes. It was on sale. Fifty per cent off.
Bibi No kidding! Is the sale still on?
Louise It ends Friday. This is failing.

They move away from each other

Bibi Well, of course it is. We're sitting on hardback chairs and you're wearing a pair of rubber storm boots! (*With a curious frown*) By the way, why do you always wear those boots in the house?
Louise Just in case.
Bibi In case of what?
Louise In case something bad happens. It's important to be wearing the right shoes.

Bibi stares at her, then decides not to pursue it. Louise suddenly gets up, kicks off her boots, pulls off her sweater, empties her wine glass and looks at Bibi with a daring smile

Couch?

Bibi Couch.

Bibi empties her wine glass, then as she gets up, kicks off her shoes and pulls off her suit jacket, Louise refills both glasses and they walk to the couch and sit down next to each other. Louise suddenly leans back against the pillows

Louise God, I'm getting drunk.
Bibi Me too.
Louise Let's just put our arms around each other and curl up a bit.

They wrap their arms around each other and curl up

Bibi This is comfy.
Louise Wrong reaction. Should we try a kiss?
Bibi Might as well. Lips?
Louise Lips.

They turn to each other and just before their lips meet both of them go limp. They lose their grip on one another and their faces miss. They sit up

Bibi What happened?
Louise We both gave in. Someone has to be the guy.
Bibi Which one?
Louise We'll flip a coin. (*She takes a coin out of a dish*) Heads or tails?
Bibi Heads.

Louise flips the coin

Louise You're the guy.
Bibi OK. Ready?

Louise nods. They take another swig of wine, put down their glasses, curl into one another's arms, then Bibi leans forward and kisses Louise full on the lips. They hold the kiss for a moment, then they slowly release each other and look away, thinking

Bibi (*glancing at Louise*) So?
Louise So what?
Bibi So what do you think?
Louise What do you think?
Bibi I asked first.

Louise I didn't hate it.
Bibi Good. I didn't hate it either.
Louise But ...
Bibi But what?
Louise (*in a rush*) But I also didn't love it. (*Pityingly*) Oh, Bibi, I'm sorry.
I know it was my idea ... Please don't blame yourself too much. If you
did, I couldn't stand it.
Bibi (*turning to look at her*) I beg your pardon ...?
Louise (*reassuringly*) You gave it your best and that's what counts.
Sexual charisma isn't everything. You're charming, you're bright and
I still think you're a very attractive person.
Bibi Are you saying I'm a lousy kisser?
Louise (*patronizingly*) Please. Bibi. Don't get defensive with me.
Bibi I'm not being defensive!
Louise Just because this meant more to you than it did to me doesn't
mean you have to ——
Bibi Meant more to me? The whole time we were kissing I was fighting
to stay awake! If your lips hadn't been pressing on mine I would have
yawned! That's how much it meant to me. Kissing you was one of the
most boring things I've ever done in my life!
Louise (*superior*) Saying unpleasant things just to get even is very, very
childish.
Bibi I'm not getting even! I don't like kissing you! It doesn't do a thing
for me! Kissing you is like kissing an envelope!

Louise stares at her, then turns away, wounded

Louise That is probably the most horrible thing anyone has ever said to
me in my life.

There is a tense silence

Bibi Louise?
Louise Yes?
Bibi I just thought of something.
Louise What?
Bibi Maybe we aren't bad kissers who love women, maybe we're good
kissers who love men.
Louise Of course! You're right!
Bibi I mean, when things are going well I love men individually, but
when I'm down on my luck I even continue to love them as a group.
Sometimes I just love seeing them moving around the streets in large
crowds in their strangely identical clothes.

Louise I even love David when he isn't smashing things. (*Frustrated*)
But why is everything so much easier between us?

Bibi Because the minute you become lovers you have to lie through your
teeth about everything! You have to flatter and defend, reassure and
shut-up ... and then, the ultimate outrage, you end up stripped naked and
defenceless in front of a person who thinks it is their moral obligation
to mankind to point out all your flaws! Do you know what we'd be
doing right now if one of us was a man?

Louise Making love.

Bibi No. We'd be up all night accusing each other of having sexual
problems.

They laugh wildly and drink more wine

Louise You know what we are, Bibi?

Bibi What?

Louise In spite of the fact that we prefer men for action, we are the very
best of friends!

Bibi (*thrilled*) Oh, I know. You're my better half! I couldn't get through
a day without you!

Louise (*thrilled*) You'll never have to! No matter what else happens in
life, we will always have each other! Oh, Bibi!

Bibi What?

Louise Why can't a man be more like a woman!

Bibi I don't know! Let's sing!

Louise What a wonderful idea! Would you like to hear my favourite
hymn?

Bibi Oh, no, please, hymns depress me. (*Excitedly*) I've got it! When I
was small my grandmother used to sing a wonderful song called *Me
and Mamie O'Rourke*!

Louise (*tenderly*) To you?

Bibi No. In the Community Gardens Bar where she went on her benders.
I thought Mamie was her best friend. Do you know it?

As Bibi sings, Louise sings softly, stumbling a bit as she learns the words

Bibi (*singing*)   East side, West side,
                              All around the town,
                              The tots play ring around rosy,
                              London Bridge is falling down.
                              Boys and girls together ...
                              Me and Mamie O'Rourke,
                              We'll trip the light fantastic
                              On the sidewalks of New York!

Louise (*emotionally*) It's so moving! Which one of us is Mamie?
Bibi We both are. You're my Mamie and I'm yours.

*They empty their glasses and refill them. During the following they end
up sprawled on the couch, their clothes half undone, skirts up to their hips*

Louise OK! Once more with feeling!
Both (*singing*)   East side, West side,
                        All around the town,
                        The tots play ring around rosy,
                        London Bridge is falling down.
                        Boys and girls together...

They smash their glasses together

            Me and Mamie O'Rourke ——

*At this moment David enters, coming through the door and slamming
it hard*

They freeze, their glasses raised

Bibi Hi, David. Have a nice night at the news-stand?
David (*appalled*) What's going on here?
Louise We're singing.

*David stares at them, disgusted, then he walks past them and goes up the
stairs*

David All I can say is, thank God the boys aren't here to see this. You
two have hit an all-time low. (*He suddenly turns back and looks at
Louise. Quietly*) Remember, Louise. Tomorrow is Sunday. Don't get
so carried away by all this merriment you forget what's going to
happen.

David and Louise stare at each other for a moment

David exits overhead

*The two women continue to sit very still, staring at the empty staircase,
Louise with fear and Bibi with a curious frown*

Bibi (*suddenly turning to Louise*) Did it ever occur to you that he never
  comes back from the news-stand carrying a paper?
Louise Yes.

They smash glasses again

Both (*singing loudly, joyfully*)
                    We'll trip the light fantastic
                    On the sidewalks of New York!

The phone suddenly rings and both women quickly turn to it

Black-out

CURTAIN

ACT II

SCENE 1

Sunday, late morning

In the laundry-room, Bibi's suitcases stand near the washing machine, open and spilling clothes. Louise comes down the stairs slowly, obviously hung over. She goes to the sink and fills the kettle with water, then plugs it in. She sits down at the table and puts her face in her hands

Clark appears in the doorway dressed as a fighter pilot, holding his helmet, nervously smoking a cigarette as he speaks

During the following, Bibi comes up the hillside steps, across the front of the stage and through the laundry-room door. She is dressed once again in her suit and hat, but looks a little the worse for wear. Just as Clark finishes his speech she walks into the room

Clark (*tensely*) When that MIG closed in on my tail and was about to fire its heat-seeking missiles, I pushed the bird to the edge of the envelope and then, out on the very edge of nothing where the sky turns black, I got him in my sights. My moment had come to give him a two-second burst on my gatling gun armed with platinum-tipped, thirty-five millimetre shells, and even though I knew that my next move was going to alter the course of history and effect the fate of the entire free world for all time ... all I could think of was you, Louise. Dancing in the moonlight with you.

Bibi Good-morning.

Louise looks up at her

Clark exits into the darkness

Louise Good-morning.
Bibi (*walking to the table and sitting down*) Did you sleep well?
Louise After the shouting stopped. Did you?
Bibi No. (*Softly, horrified*) On my way home, I caught him in the garage walling up two dead hamsters. I was up all night.

The kettle whistles and Louise gets up, goes to the counter and makes two cups of tea

Bibi (*looking at her hopefully*) Did you ever find out who called?

Louise No. I told you last night, after David picked up the extension and screamed, "The next time you call at this hour, you filthy roach, I'll cut your heart out with a rusty can-opener," the person hung up.

Bibi And they didn't call back?

Louise (*carrying the tea carefully to the table and sitting down again*) They never call back.

They sip their tea carefully for a moment

Louise (*looking at Bibi*) He called me an unfit mother.

Bibi (*helpfully*) That's not so bad. He usually calls you an alcoholic.

Louise That's because I never used to drink.

Bibi How could you? Until you met me, you thought having a good time was the same as going insane.

Louise He ran out at two o'clock.

Bibi Gone all night?

Louise nods

Where'd he go?

Louise The news-stand.

Bibi A-ha. (*Suddenly*) Have you ever actually seen him sleep standing up?

Louise (*distractedly*) No, but he insists he can.

Bibi Any parting words?

Louise Yes. He said he wouldn't be back until this afternoon to dispose of the last of the architectural atrocities. When I objected he said he had to do it. He said it was his destiny and no man of genius can afford to resist his destiny for any reason. He said it was an outrage against all that was fine and beautiful in life and that if he left it intact simply to please me he would be betraying his integrity and he would lose all self-respect.

Bibi He's such a tease.

They sip their tea

(*Suddenly, anxiously*) You're sure the phone didn't even ring once since last night? Maybe it rang and you didn't answer it in time?

Louise shakes her head "no"

Well.
Louise Well what?
Bibi (*sombrely*) I suppose I should start making the soup.
Louise (*softly, anxiously*) The soup? Why the soup?
Bibi Because it looks like tragedy for both of us. Yesterday's lunch keeps getting longer and longer and it doesn't look like Uncle Felix is going to bite the dust in the near——
Louise (*slapping her hands over her ears*) Don't say bite the dust! (*She lowers her hands, horrified*) It makes me think of his dentures. There's something so vulnerable about a person's dentures, especially when they're outside the mouth.
Bibi I know what you mean. All those little chips and stains tell quite a tale of eating, smoking, chatting, brushing, flossing, grinding ——
Louise Stop! You're making me sick and I'm sick enough with self-loathing and guilt.
Bibi (*compassionately*) Of course you are. How could you not be, waiting for that poor old man to die? Let's try and keep busy, Louise. Neither one of us will make it through the day otherwise.
Louise Yes, you're right. We have to keep ourselves distracted or we'll go insane. I'll do some research on the vests and you make ... the soup.

Louise goes to the easy chair and sits down with the stack of magazines. Bibi takes her hat off and tosses it down on the counter. She pulls a soup pot out of a cabinet, puts it down next to her hat, then as she turns toward the refrigerator she suddenly stops and puts her face in her hands

Bibi (*in tears*) He's not coming, Louise, is he?
Louise You can't be sure.
Bibi It's going to be like all the other times I was foolish enough to give my heart with abandon, to love without any thought for myself.
Louise He's only two hours late this time.
Bibi But it's the second time! And he could have called!
Louise Maybe that was him last night!
Bibi He could have called back this morning!
Louise Call him.
Bibi I did.
Louise What happened.
Bibi No answer. Oh, Louise. Do you think he made it up with his girlfriend?
Louise It's a possibility.
Bibi I'll die! I'll die!

Louise But there are hundreds of other possibilities too!

Bibi Like what?

Louise Maybe she threatened to commit suicide if he went away with you.

Bibi Of course! Why didn't I think of that!

Louise Maybe at this very moment she's standing on the topmost, outer ledge of a tall building. A crowd stands below shouting, "Jump! Jump!" She teeters on the edge, clutching a window ledge, confused, heartbroken, unable to see a way out of her misery. She begs him to forget you, but this is a promise he cannot make. Instead, he kneels at the window, supported by a Catholic priest, pleading, reminding her that she is young, her life is all in front of her, she will love again and all this will just be a bad memory if only she will take those few, short steps back from oblivion.

Bibi No wonder he hasn't called!

Louise It would be criminally irresponsible to leave her alone for even a moment!

Bibi Do you really think that's the problem?

Louise I do!

Bibi I don't.

Louise Well, you could be right.

Bibi sits down at the table with a small, tragic smile on her face

Bibi That was kind of you, Louise, but I don't have to be shielded from reality. I can take it. I'm used to this.

Louise You must be by now. It happens to you so often.

Bibi He's just doing what they all do, isn't he?

Louise What's that?

Bibi Hiding.

Louise Hiding? From what?

Bibi Me.

Louise You ...? (*The light breaks*) Of course! What choice does he have? (*Triumphantly*) He's threatened by you.

Bibi Has it ever been different?

Louise Never. Men are always threatened by you.

Bibi He's hiding from the turbulent and unfamiliar emotions I arouse in him.

Louise Very few people have your emotional courage, Bibi.

Bibi It's sad, isn't it? We were only together once, for twenty minutes in a public place, and already he's running away from making a commitment. Oh, but I'm a fool, Louise, and I always have been when it comes to love. I've always let passion rule my life rather than self-interest or common sense. I've never been able to resist the wild impulses of my heart, no matter where they've led me, and because of that I've paid a high price. (*She looks at her*) I'm alone Louise. I'm deeply, deeply alone.

Louise You always have me, Bibi.

Bibi (*looking away, shaking her head sadly*) No, Louise, I'm alone. I'm one of a kind and that road is a hard one. Do you know why I'm not like all the rest? (*She looks at her intensely*) Because most people are sheep, most people live in fear of passion. Right now he's off in a room somewhere, struggling with his fear. Chances are fear will win, it usually does. He'll hide for a few weeks, then make a swift, late-night visit to me because he is overwhelmed with love and desire, then he'll vanish again for another month. It will be painful for both of us, but I won't let the pain defeat the wild fool in me, and someday, someday I'll meet someone with a wayward heart like mine. Someday I will love a man who is as free from fear as I am, Louise, and when I do it will be without memory of disappointment, I'll do it as if it is the first time, the only time, the right time!

Louise Oh, Bibi! I admire you so much! Your courage! Your heart! Your imagination!

Bibi (*brightly*) And who knows? Maybe she is attempting suicide after all! (*She gets up and briskly walks to the refrigerator*)

Louise returns to the easy chair

David enters across the back of the stage, past the windows

Bibi (*cheerfully*) So, what's it to be? Chicken or vegetable?

Louise Chicken's more comforting.

David comes through the door as Bibi pulls a bunch of carrots out of the refrigerator

David Vegetable's faster.

The two women look up, startled

Bibi You're early.

David You're here again.

Bibi (*quickly dropping the carrots on the counter*) I'm going.

Louise (*quickly standing up*) No, you're not! Stay right where you are! (*Coldly*) I want a witness.

Bibi (*grabbing her hat and starting for the door; frantically*) A witness to what? I think the two of you need a little time alone together to talk things over, or better yet maybe you should get into some kind of program for the maritally handicapped or ——

David (*looking hard at Bibi*) Louise is right. An occasion like this calls for a witness. Sit down please, Bibi.

Bibi stands frozen, looking from one to the other

(*Loudly*) I said sit!

Bibi quickly walks to a chair and sits down. David and Louise stare at each other in silence for a moment

I think you know why I've come home, don't you?

Louise Yes.

David Is there anything you want to say to me about it?

Louise Yes.

David What's that?

Louise I'm not going to let you do this.

David I expected you to say that. I will not be stopped.

Bibi (*turning quickly to Louise; with a sharp hiss*) Lou-ise!

David (*sharply*) Don't talk! You're just a witness!

Bibi Excuse me!

David (*turning to her impatiently*) What now?

Bibi I'd like a glass of water, please.

David Well, get up and get one. Why are you telling me about it?

Bibi (*walking to the sink*) Because you're the one who told me to sit. (*As she fills a glass with water, she quickly turns to Louise, her back to David. With a sharp hiss*) Sharpen up! Felix has potential! Don't threaten, negotiate!

David What was that?!

Bibi (*going back to her chair*) Nothing.

David (*amazed*) You can do it in front of me and I still can't catch you! (*To Louise*) What were you suggesting, Louise? That you're going to stop me? How do you intend to do that?

Louise I would like to make a deal.

Bibi (*with a relieved shriek*) At last!

David (*to Bibi*) Will you please settle down? (*To Louise*) A deal? What kind of a deal?

Louise Very soon now I will have something you desperately want.

David (*startled*) A new chainsaw?

Louise No. I will have something you haven't seen for a long time, David, something you love the feel of, the smell of, the colour of, something you like to hold in your hand.

David (*confused*) A persimmon ...?

Louise I'm not talking fruit and vegetables, pal, I'm talking cash! Hard currency, lettuce, spondulicks, wedge! I will have the readies to build pods!

David (*sneering*) Where would you get money?

Louise I don't want to discuss that. It's slightly sordid.

Bibi Well, not exactly sordid, but definitely unattractive.

Louise You do want to build pods, David, don't you?

David (*suspiciously*) I don't want to answer that until I know what's going on here. I sense a trap.

Louise Not a trap, a trade. Do you want the money or not?

David (*cautiously*) Of course I want the money.

Louise Then are you open to negotiation?

David That depends.

Louise On what?

David Your terms.

Bibi Oh, thank God! You're negotiating!

Louise Ssshhh! (*To David*) I have only one demand. Leave what's mine standing.

David And in return, what do I get?

Louise The money. All of it. It's yours.

David (*looking at her, then folding his arms*) OK, Louise. You've got yourself a deal.

Louise (*thrilled*) I do?

David On one condition.

Louise (*tensing up*) What?

David That you tell me when this money is arriving and where you are getting it.

Louise It's arriving soon.

David How soon?

Louise Maybe by tomorrow. Wednesday at the latest. Will you at least wait until Wednesday?

David Yes, but only if you'll tell me where it's coming from.

Louise I can't do that.

David I won't trust you if you don't.

Louise I can't.

Bibi (*leaping up from her seat*) Tell him!

Louise Quiet, Bibi! Stay out of this!

Bibi How can I? You're blowing it!

David Where's it coming from, Louise?
Louise Never mind.
David I have to know or I'm going up those stairs now.
Louise I can't tell you.
Bibi Tell him!
Louise No!
Bibi Why?
Louise I have my reasons!

David looks at them both, then slowly walks to the stairs. Their eyes are glued to him. He hesitates for a second, then slides the sledge-hammer out from under the steps

David Are you sure you can't tell me?
Louise No! I can't!
Bibi You must!
Louise I can't!

David starts up the stairs with the sledge-hammer

If you touch it, no money!
David Tell me.
Louise No!
Bibi (*shrieking*) Uncle Felix!
David (*stopping and turning to look at them with disgust; contemptuously*) Uncle Felix?
Louise (*to Bibi*) I told you to stay out of it! He would have folded if you'd kept quiet!
David All this trading has been over your inheritance from your Uncle Felix?
Louise (*walking quickly to the stairs; pleading*) I know it's hard to believe, but he's fading this time! He can't last the night!
David He does that once a month.
Louise He's ninety-two.
David I'm sorry, Louise. I know this is going to be hard on you, but there are some things that are more important to a man than his wife's feelings. When you married me, you also married my ideas.

He starts up the stairs. Bibi races up next to Louise

Louise (*with a furious cry*) This isn't just your house, you know, it's mine too, and you're not the only one with ideas!

He keeps climbing in silence

(*Frantically*) And what will you do when it's gone?! What will you do
when there's nothing left to destroy? (*Desperately, frightened*) How
will we go on? If you do this we'll all be lost, we'll all be ——

The sudden ringing of the phone cuts her off and she races for it

David exits overhead

(*Ripping up the receiver; hysterically*) Hallo? ... He did? ... Are you
sure? ... (*Her body goes limp and she sinks into a chair, sobbing*)
Oh, thank God. ... Thank God. ... Yes, yes. ... Thank God. ... Just
thank God. ...
Bibi (*frantically*) Felix?

*Louise nods as she blindly hangs up the phone, unable to speak through
her sobs. Bibi starts running up the stairs*

(*Shouting*) David! Stop! Felix ——

*She is cut off by an enormous crash overhead. Both women freeze as
rubble comes tumbling down the stairs. Pause. Louise slowly stands up
and walks to the stairs. She stares at the rubble as Bibi comes slowly down
the stairs, then she sinks to her knees and touches it*

Louise (*in tears*) My fireplace! My beautiful imitation Adams fireplace!
First home, now hearth ... gone! All those Christmases to come where
I imagined we would sit in front of a cheerful blaze, opening our
presents, dressed in gaily coloured bathrobes made of natural fibre, just
like you see in Polaroid ads showing normal American families having
holiday fun. All gone.

Pause. Bibi puts a comforting hand on Louise's shoulder

Bibi Get up, Louise. I'll make some chicken soup and then we'll sit down
and revise the plan.
Louise (*slowly turning to look at her; dazed*) Revise the plan ...?
Bibi Yes. It's the only way, in times of trouble, to get your feet back on
the ground and revive your spirits. You can't just wallow in the pain,
you've got to pull yourself up by the bootstraps, look the experience in
the face, assess the damage and, if necessary, revise your life plan to
accommodate it. I know this all looks grim at the moment, but now that
Felix is gone ——

Louise Gone? Felix isn't gone.

Bibi Well, I know you still believe in life after death, but ——

Louise (*shouting*) Felix isn't dead! He pulled through! Felix's dentures are continuing the tale! Felix rallied, got a new lease, slipped the grip of the reaper! (*She sobs*) Felix is on his way home as we speak and I wished him dead for two whole days! I can't believe I did such a terrible thing!

Bibi I can't either.

Louise It was your idea to do it!

Bibi So. I didn't make you do it, did I? Anyway, that's not important now. What's important is to calm down, examine what happened and plan for the future.

Louise No.

Bibi No?

Louise No. I won't.

Bibi But, Louise, you must. How can we accept all this suffering if we don't understand the reasons for it? How can we go on without something to go on to? Where would we be, Louise, without the plan?

Louise Exactly where we are! Living out the best years of our lives in a cellar!

Bibi Oh, stop exaggerating. You spend lots of time in the garden, I go to the restaurant, we make innumerable trips to the market, the dentist, the cleaners, the ——

Louise Life is passing us by, Bibi! Our plans are meaningless! They don't make anything start and they don't make anything stop! They don't make anything happen at all!

Bibi Well, no, I suppose they don't, but then plans don't make things happen, they just give you some idea of what to do in case something does happen. Anyway, our plans are about the future, they're made up of hopes and dreams and ——

Louise Bald-faced lies!

Bibi stiffens. They stare at each other

Here we sit, year after year, scheming and plotting and examining our lives, busily avoiding anything that will reveal what we really are! A couple of cowards who spend all their time lying through their teeth rather than do anything hard!

Bibi (*amazed*) You don't think any of this has been hard?

Louise No. How could this be hard? We invented it. And if by some freak chance the outside world dares to enter here, we transform the event, as if by magic, into something of our own making, truth becomes lie and we're safe again. There may be suffering, but there will be no surprises.

Bibi stares at her, then turns and quickly walks to the counter. She picks up a peeler and the carrots and starts peeling

Bibi I'll just make a little soup while you calm down and then we can talk.

Louise (*advancing on her*) I don't want to calm down! I want to do something hard, Bibi!

Bibi How can we do anything while you're in this hysterical state?

Louise I want to talk straight instead of talking lies! Somebody's got to finally tell the truth around here!

Bibi I don't know about you, Louise, but the one thing I never do is lie!

Louise Oh, yeah? What about the jerks?

Bibi I beg your pardon?

Louise The jerks! The endless string of moronic strangers you fall in love with at the drop of a hat! My God, the lies we have to tell about them!

Bibi (*keeping her back turned, nervously scraping the carrots*) A few deep breaths, a nice glass of water and you'll be yourself again in a minute.

Louise Remember the guy who used to wear leisure suits and make rude noises during dinner?

Bibi Gardening is an excellent release during periods of emotional stress and I did notice that your johnny jump-ups needed attention.

Louise We decided that the reason he only came to see you a couple of hours every three or four weeks was not because he wasn't in love with you, but because he was a latent homosexual who was threatened by your sexuality. And remember what we said about the gas station attendant who stole your portable typewriter and your Mix-master?

Bibi These carrots are not fresh.

Louise We said he was so threatened by your superior intelligence he had to steal to establish dominance. And the married guy who only saw you on his lunch hours? We said he didn't leave his wife for you because he was looking for a mother and was deeply threatened by your independence. Independence, hah! You used to wait for him every other Thursday wearing nothing but a salad niçoise!

Bibi I really think you should be sharing this moment of catharsis with your husband. I didn't tear your house down, he did.

Louise And here we are, once again inventing lies about a man who hasn't shown up! The guy from the check-out counter isn't threatened by you, Bibi, he's not here because he's got better things to do and do you know why? He's a total stranger who can barely remember your name!

Bibi stiffens, then slowly turns to face Louise

Bibi Oh, really.

Louise Yes, really. Over the years we've told a hundred different lies to cover one sorry little truth.

Pause. They stare at each other

You haven't been loved in so long you think being loved is the same as being used! How can any man respect you when you don't respect yourself? They know you'll accept little, they offer you nothing and you take it. Over and over and over. (*Upset*) I can't lie anymore, Bibi, I just can't do it. If I've hurt you, I'm sorry ... I don't really know how you feel since I don't have that problem with men. They always seem to want me more than I want them.

Bibi stares at her, then suddenly tosses the peeler into the sink

Bibi What kind of men are you talking about, Louise? Men like cod-faced Clark?

Louise Cod-faced who?

Clark appears in the doorway wearing his smoking-jacket

Clark Watch out, Louise. Jealousy of our love has made her dangerous.

Louise Just what do you mean by that vicious remark?

Bibi I mean I saw the pictures of the boy-wonder. I mean this man who wants you more than you want him looks so much like a fish I want to poach him! I mean he's so damn ugly he couldn't get close enough to me to steal my Mix-master! How's that for the truth? I hope it wasn't too painful for you, dear, but then I wouldn't know. I've never been into ichthyology.

Clark Pity her, Louise. She has never known a passionate love like ours.

Louise (*coldly superior*) I'm sorry for you. I really am. You're bitter because no-one has ever loved you the way Clark loved me! I would have married him if David hadn't swept me off my feet!

Bibi Lie! You tricked David into marrying you because Clark was such a dull-witted bore. David said that when he first met you, you weren't in love with Clark, you were in a coma!

Clark (*alarmed*) Don't respond, Louise! There might be no way back!

Louise (*furiously*) I tricked David into marrying me! That's absolute slander!

Bibi You sent him to the store to buy a jar of pickled beets and while he was gone you announced your engagement to your family! When he got back he was too embarrassed to say you were lying so you got married!

Louise That is a vicious interpretation of a rather silly little story!

Bibi As for Clark, David met him, remember? He told me the sound of Clark's voice would work better than ether during major surgery and that he had the sense of humour of an aphid. I think the only reason you were with him was because he was so stupid he thought you were smart!

Clark (*panicky*) Let it go, Louise! Let it go!

Louise Clark is not stupid! He's a medical man, with an air force background!

Bibi He runs a health food store next to an air force base!

As Louise stiffens and stares angrily at Bibi, Clark begins to vanish back into the gloom

Clark Be careful, Louise ... if you keep going there might be no way back ...

He exits

Louise (*with a cold smile*) It's difficult to pay any attention to what you say, Bibi. After all, you live the biggest lie of all, don't you?

Pause

Bibi Don't say it, Louise. I'm warning you.

Louise I'm going to say it.

Bibi If you do, it's the end.

Louise You can't stop me now.

Bibi Don't do it.

Louise (*triumphantly, loudly*) Jane Goodall did not make it on her contacts!

Bibi stares at her, then turns, walks rapidly to the cabinet, picks up her hat and pins it on with shaky hands

Bibi I happen to have done quite a bit of research on that particular subject and ——

Louise And you don't know a damn thing about it! You twist what you read to fit what you want to think!

Bibi (*walking to the door*) You're just saying this because you're jealous of my fulfilling future in science when all you have to look forward to is a life spent cleaning pods that cockroaches wouldn't even move into!

Louise I have my own work too, thank you.

Bibi Oh, right! Louise, the great, untried genius who sits around talking about all the brilliant things she has never done!

Louise (*withering*) How about you, Bibi? When you're an animal behaviourist what will you study? The robin redbreast? The domestic cat? The bluebird of happiness? You're not an animal behaviourist and you never will be! You're just a cook.

Bibi (*in tears*) That just explains your revolting salads made from iceberg lettuce and bottled dressing! (*Furiously*) And what about your biggest lie, oh great truth-lover? Tell me, when David goes to the news-stand, does he ever buy a paper or magazine?

Louise What?

Bibi Answer. Does he?

Louise (*disdainfully*) No. He doesn't. But I don't see what that has to do with ——

Bibi Does he spend several hours a day at the news-stand? Answer!

Louise Yes.

Bibi Does he spend most of his evenings at the news-stand after he's been there all day? Speak up!

Louise (*uneasily*) Yes, he does, but what are you ——

Bibi And does he occasionally spend all night at the news-stand?

Louise Just what are getting at, Bibi? What disgusting thing are you insinuating now?

Bibi It's obvious to anyone with half a brain that David is having an affair!

Louise freezes. Pause. Tears fill her eyes

Louise How could you say something so cruel and vile after all the suffering I've endured?

Bibi Oh, you and your suffering. You love every minute of it, Louise, because it keeps David here and do you know why you want him here? Because you're afraid you're not so smart after all. You're afraid you're not half as good as you think you are. You're afraid to go out there and take your chances like the rest of us. It's much safer to be victimized by David the monster and dream of your genius rather than go out there and discover you're just ordinary. Face it, Dr Frankenstein, David is your creature, for better or for worse.

Bibi spins around and races out the door in tears. She runs across the front of the stage, up the hillside steps and exits

Clark starts singing off stage and Louise slowly turns to look at the doorway under the stairs

*As he sings, Clark enters and dances his way into view. He looks exactly
the same, except his face is that of a large, ugly fish*

Clark (*off; cheerfully singing*)
>Down in the meadow
>In a little bitty pool
>Swam three little fishies
>And a mama fishy too,
>"Fwim," said the mama fishy,
>"Fwim if you can,"
>And they fwam and they fwam
>All over the dam ...
>Boop boop dittem dottem whattem chu!
>Boop boop dittem dottem whattem chu!
>Boop boop dittem dottem whattem chu!
>And they fwam and they fwam
>All over the dam!

*Louise stares at him with horror as he finishes his song and leans in the
doorway*

(*In whiny, nasal tones*) Have you seen my dietary supplements, honey?
My allergies are really acting up today. I'm under so much stress at the
health food store it's affecting my immune system and I'm feeling
really toxic. If I don't watch out I could end up with another intestinal
yeast infection!

*Slapping her hands over her ears to shut him out, Louise quickly turns her
back on him and sinks into a chair with a great wail of despair*

(*In whiny, nasal tones*) Well, I warned you, didn't I?

Black-out

SCENE 2

Sunday. Early evening

*The darkening sky shows traces of the setting sun, the colour of which
intensifies throughout this scene until, at the end, everything outside the
laundry-room is bathed in the last brilliant light of the day. The lamps are
already lit inside the laundry-room. The rubble is not cleaned up and two*

*large duffle bags sit next to the door. Bibi's suitcases are packed and
shoved off in a corner. Louise is on the phone, listening with a stricken
face to it ringing at the other end. She finally hangs up and walks to the
dressmaker's dummy. Glancing occasionally at a magazine spread out
on a chair, she pins small circles of brown paper to the dummy. We hear
footsteps above the stage. She glances anxiously at the top of the stairs*

David enters and comes downstairs carrying the sledge hammer

*As soon as he appears she quickly goes back to the dummy, never looking
up. He watches her as he slips the hammer back under the steps, then
walks over to her. She ignores him. He glances at the magazine with a
frown*

David Why do you read this trash?
Louise It's not trash, it's a paramilitary trade magazine and I'm not
    reading it for pleasure, I'm using it to get information.
David About what? The best method for fitting a dismembered body into
    a suitcase?
Louise No. About which parts of the anatomy tend to eat lead during
    sniper attacks.

He gives her a glance, then walks to the table and sits down. Pause

David Where's Bibi? Heading for the border at last?
Louise I haven't the faintest idea.

Pause

David You're so quiet. (*Pause*) I'm surprised. (*Pause*) I thought you'd
    be angry. (*Pause*) Don't you have anything to say to me?
Louise No.
David (*disappointed*) I'm surprised.
Louise You've already said that.

*He watches her for a moment, then gets up, paces restlessly to the
refrigerator, opens it and looks inside, then shuts it again and leans
against it, looking at her*

David (*impatiently*) Are you going to pin paper on that dummy all night?
Louise Yes.

Pause, then he restlessly walks back to the table and sinks into a chair

David (*abruptly, provocatively*) Well, Louise, I have to say I'm impressed. (*Pause*) I'm not only impressed, I'm pleased. (*Pause*) I'm pleased to see you're being mature about all this. You're taking it all very well.
Louise You think so?
David Yes, I do, Louise.
Louise Well, you're dead wrong. I'm not. As a matter of fact, I'm not taking it at all.
David (*sighing with satisfaction*) I knew it. I knew this period of calm was just a prelude to a fight.
Louise I don't want a fight.
David Yes, you do.
Louise No, I don't. It's too small-time. I want something more exciting than a fight, something more fulfilling, something equal to what you did today, something with deeper and more soul-satisfying results.
David Like what?
Louise Revenge. (*Suddenly*) You look tired, David. You've had a gruelling day ... maybe you should go someplace and relax for a while.
David Go someplace? Where do you suggest I go?
Louise Oh, I don't know ... someplace where you feel wanted and understood, where you feel happy, fulfilled and appreciated ... someplace where they cater to your every need ... someplace like — the news-stand. After all, you have such strong feelings about the news.
David (*confused*) The news? I don't have any feelings about the news.
Louise Maybe, but I bet you have very deep feelings for the news-stand. I think you have a passionate attachment to the news-stand, I think you're devoted to it, I bet you're even a little in love with the news-stand.
David Are you feeling all right?
Louise I've never felt better! A sharp, almost electric energy is shooting through my body, filling me with wild exhilaration! I feel light and quick, so quick I could defy gravity if I wanted to! Some people would call this being on the edge of hysteria, but I don't. I call it feeling fine, David. I call it feeling ... powerful!
David Yeah, well ... maybe I will take a run down to the news-stand after all.
Louise (*working on the dummy*) I thought you would. Goodbye.

He hesitates, then shrugs slightly and heads for the door

David Goodbye.
Louise Oh, by the way, would you do me a little favour on your way out? Take those duffle bags with you?

He notices them for the first time and looks back at her

David Take them where?

Louise Wherever you're going. You're going to need a change of clothes.

David What is this?

Louise You're going to need your clothes. As soon as you walk out that door, which I cannot wait for you to do, you will not be living here anymore. (*Chattily*) Most of your shirts are there, but the green plaid needed some buttons sewn on so you'll have to get it later in the week when you stop by to talk to the boys about our impending divorce.

They stare at each other, then David takes a few steps back into the room

David Is this a joke?

Louise I just delivered the punch line and neither one of us is laughing.

David (*walking further back into the room*) Are you insane, Louise? We've been married for ten years!

Louise So?

David So people don't just end ten-year marriages by leaving duffle bags in the doorway!

Louise I admit it's a novel approach, but why dawdle? Why not just pick up your bags and hit the road without indulging in a lot of pointless chit-chat about where we went wrong? We went wrong. That's enough for me.

David Well, it's not enough for me! And it won't be enough for our children either! Some explanation is called for!

Louise I told you to leave that fireplace alone!

David You want a divorce because I ripped out a fireplace?

Louise (*shouting*) That wasn't just a fireplace! (*Softly, lethally*) It was my line, David. I drew a line and told you not to cross it. I watched you, month after month, drawing closer, your eye always on it. You couldn't wait to get to it. I warned you it would be dangerous, but you had to do it and now I will take that stand you were dying for me to take, but I don't think you're going to like it because it's the end of the game. I want you out, I want you to take that long overdue hike to nowhere and if you're confused about how to do it, just repeat after me, "Feets don't fail me now."

He stares at her

David (*after a moment; stubbornly*) I can't leave. You need me too much.

Louise Need you? For what?
David This house isn't safe. You need me to put it back together. You can't be left here alone.
Louise (*exploding*) I've been here alone for three years! You only appear during periods of demolition! I don't need you to make this place safe, I'll do it myself.
David (*superior*) Oh, please, Louise. How do you expect to do that?
Louise How else? (*Fiercely*) The hard way! I'll get down on my hands and knees and put back every single thing you ripped out! I'll rebuild until my hands bleed, until my eyesight fades, until my bones turn to jelly with exhaustion! I'll spend every waking moment on it and when I'm sleeping I'll dream about it! And when I'm finished, when all the little doors and windows and staircases and walls are back in place, do you know what I'll do then?
David What?
Louise (*threateningly*) I will cover the backs of all the chairs and couches with doilies!

He stares at her, then quickly turns and heads for the door

David That's it, I'm out of here. I'll come back in the morning when you've had time to come to your senses.
Louise (*sweetly*) But where will you stay tonight, dear?
David (*with a wary glance*) I don't know.
Louise I do.
David (*turning to look at her*) What do you mean? Where?
Louise (*bitter, pointedly*) The "news-stand".
David (*stiffening; staring at her; then suddenly letting his breath out*) You know.
Louise Beast! (*She walks to the easy chair and sits down*) I was only guessing.

He stares at her, then walks back to the table and sinks into a chair

David (*shattered*) I'm sorry, Louise ... I don't know how it happened ...
Louise And I don't want to.
David (*desperately*) I wasn't looking for it ... it's just that she gave me something ... something I needed ...
Louise I know. A house with walls. How long has it been going on?
David Six months and two days.
Louise (*taken aback*) You have anniversaries?
David (*shattered*) She likes to celebrate things ... firsts ... like the first time I drove her car ... she gives me presents ...

Louise Do you love her?

David (*tortured, with a helpless shrug*) I don't know ... she's different from you ... she doesn't complain all the time ...

Louise (*softly, lethally*) Watch what you say, David. Don't forget that I have been reading the kind of magazine that has inadvertently taught me how to kill.

David (*suddenly, frustrated*) How can you even ask me about love? Love's a luxury for people like us! Finding a way out is more important than love! (*Tortured*) You were right about the fireplace. I was obsessed with it ... nothing else had the same value ... for weeks at a time it's all I thought about ... saving it for the end was so hard. (*Desperately*) Be grateful I did it, Louise. If I hadn't the destruction would have escalated ... eventually I would have had to start on the outside of the house ... then I would have attacked the garden ... God only knows where it would have stopped! In my state, I probably would have ended up going after the neighbours' houses.

Louise (*in deep admiration*) There's a lot about you I'm suspicious of, David, but I really respect your commitment to your aesthetic principles.

David (*exploding*) This wasn't about aesthetics! It was about your protected life! I hate your protected life!

Louise My protected life! You call living in a laundry-room under a great pile of rubble a protected life?

David Yes! You never have to be the bully, you never have to be the person who makes the decisions that ruin our lives, you never have to be the failed genius! That's who I am! It's easy for you to look good, you never have to do anything except occupy the moral high ground and endure my mistakes! You're always the victim, "the injured party". You never do anything so you can't do anything wrong! Try being the person who does the things that you and Bibi judge and condemn twenty times a day and see how much you like it!

Louise Don't drag Bibi into this!

David Drag her into this! You, Bibi and I are Siamese triplets! Without her we would have had to tell the truth a long time ago and for a while anything seemed better than that. (*Softly, destroyed*) Anything seemed better than admitting to myself that I'm probably out of work not because I'm a genius, but because I'm just not very good ... that I build pods as an act of revenge rather than an act of creation.

She looks at him with sudden compassion, almost as if she's seeing him for the first time in a long time

Louise David?

David Yes.

Pause

Louise You're good.
David (*looking at her with surprise; gratefully*) Thank you, Louise. You haven't said that in so many years I assumed it wasn't true.
Louise I couldn't say it. We don't talk.
David No. Of course not. Why would we do such a foolishly dangerous thing? (*Wondering*) But still, just think of all the things we might have said if we had been talking.
Louise (*mimicking*) It's a nice day, isn't it? For some people. What's that supposed to mean? Nothing you'd understand.
David You're right. Talking was out of the question.
Louise I can only talk to Bibi.
David (*with melancholy*) You have no idea how lonely the sound of your voices makes me feel. When I'm in the house you talk in whispers, when I'm gone you talk openly and when I'm in the room you talk behind my back ... you never stop talking. (*With intense longing*) What do you find to talk about all the time? I've always wondered.
Louise Even if I told you, you wouldn't get it.
David Why not?
Louise Because it's not about what we say ... it's just about doing it.

They sit staring at each other for a moment

David We're talking now.
Louise Yeah. I can't think of anything to say. (*She pauses, helpless*)

Pause

David I don't want to go, Louise. (*Pause*) But I'm warning you, if you insist on it, I will do it.

She stares at him, her nerve momentarily shaken, remembering how she loved him once, then she takes a deep breath

Louise I insist on it.
David (*unnerved*) Are you sure? Are you absolutely sure? I mean, if you're not, you'd better say so now because when I go out that door I might not be coming back. Think about it, Louise.
Louise I've been thinking about it for three years.
David (*shattered*) How on earth did we end up here?

Louise (*lost*) I don't know. We were happy in the beginning once you forgave me for tricking you into marriage.

David (*with sudden suspicion*) Have you met someone else ...?

Louise (*sweeping her arm around the room*) Here?!

David I'm going to view this as a temporary separation, Louise.

Louise You can view it any way you want as long as you go and don't come back.

He hesitates, then gets up, slowly walks to the door and picks up the duffle bags. She gets to her feet as he turns to look back at her

David In that case, I'm leaving.

Louise Oh, no, you're not! I'm kicking you out! You're the one who's being left, not me!

David (*superior*) Does that really matter?

Louise Yes. It does. (*She pauses and takes a deep, emotional breath*) So long, David.

David (*staring at her; heartbroken*) So long, Louise. (*He hesitates a moment longer, then he walks out the door. He stops to look at her through the windows. Hopefully*) Do you think we'll at least end up friends ... ?

She stares at him, then smiles sweetly and shakes her head

Louise Not a chance in hell.

He looks taken aback, then turns and exits

The moment he disappears Louise starts pacing back and forth across the room

During the following, Bibi enters and comes slowly down the hillside steps. She walks across the stage to the laundry-room door

Do not panic, Louise. You got what you wanted, now learn to live with it. (*With a frightened moan*) But I'm alone, no-one loves me and I'm alone ... (*Sternly*) You're free. Your life belongs to you now and it will be what you make of it. Stop being so pathetic. (*Frightened*) But I'm afraid ... what if I can't make anything of it? What if there's nothing to me? (*Sternly*) You're being self-indulgent. There's no time for doubt now, no time for second thoughts. You have work to do. (*Her eyes fill with tears*) What's work compared to love? I won't see that unguarded look in his eyes first thing in the morning, before he remembers how bad things got ... she'll see that look now ...

Bibi appears in the doorway. She glances around the room, looking for the person Louise has been talking to

(*Trying to regain control*) Don't think about them. Just take it one day at a time, if you take it one day at a time everything will be ... (*She sees Bibi*) Oh, God! Bibi! (*She rushes over to her*) Oh, Bibi! Thank God you're here! I was afraid you might have gone to Mexico without talking to me. Will you ever forgive me for those terrible things I said to you?

Bibi No.

Louise No ...?

Bibi What I mean is we said so much, Louise. When you say that much apologies don't matter anymore.

Louise (*apprehensively*) Then what does?

Bibi The truth. (*Puzzled*) Who were you talking to just now?

Louise (*sitting down at the table*) You.

Bibi Me?

Louise Yeah, but I was being both people.

Bibi That's called talking to yourself.

Louise It's over, Bibi. It's finally over between David and me.

Bibi I know that. I was here when he took down the fireplace, remember?

Louise I don't mean that. I mean our marriage is over. I kicked him out.

Bibi (*horrified*) You kicked him out?

Louise Duffle bags and all. I'm sending the sledge-hammer by messenger.

Bibi (*aghast*) You didn't do it because of that stupid thing I said when I walked out, did you?

Louise Yes.

Bibi But I was only guessing about the affair!

Louise No, you weren't. Who sleeps standing up? We both knew, I just didn't want to.

Bibi Oh my God! Why did I say such a horrible thing? Why?

Louise Because I was saying horrible things to you. Oh, Bibi, none of it was true.

Bibi Yes, it was. All of it. Unnecessarily cruel, perhaps, but definitely true.

Louise No, it wasn't! What do I know about Jane Goodall's career moves?

Bibi Nothing, and neither do I. After I went home, I looked through my Jane Goodall scrapbook and you were right, of course. I twisted what little information I had to make myself feel good. Jane Goodall did not make it on her contacts.

Louise Well, so what! Just because she didn't doesn't mean you can't!

Bibi I don't have any contacts.

Louise You'll get them. Sooner or later Jane Goodall will answer all those letters ...

Bibi No! (*Pause*) Don't start the lies again, Louise. I'm just starting to get used to the truth.

Louise Lies and dreams aren't the same, Bibi. You have a dream and ——

Bibi I'm afraid of wild animals!

Louise You'll get over that.

Bibi And I don't like to travel and I hate camping out.

Louise Well, that does put a different light on things.

Bibi I'm not a scientist, Louise, I'm just a cook.

Louise Not just a cook! I only said that to hurt you! You're a great cook! (*She stares at her, then suddenly smiles with a growing hope and excitement*) You know, Bibi, I was terrified when David walked out that door, but now I'm beginning to feel excited about the future. It's going to be completely different.

Bibi It'll be different all right. (*With a sudden sigh*) I'm really going to miss David. I've always been very uneasy around happy people, they seem so phoney, but you two! We were all so miserable together it was like being part of a family.

Louise Don't waste time looking back! This isn't the end of something, it's the beginning of a new era, an era of hope and light after years of despair and darkness!

Bibi (*cautiously; worried*) What do you mean?

Louise (*getting up and pacing*) Well, there's no reason why you have to live in that pet burial ground. Now that David's gone you can live here! The boys would love it, it would be like going on that trip to Wisconsin forever! Obviously, sooner or later one or both of us will fall in love and we'll have to rearrange things, but for the moment, why not? And between the two of us ... well, the sky's the limit, isn't it? I'll concentrate on getting the vests on to the market, maybe we could even open a restaurant! What do you think of that?

Bibi stares at her

Well, don't just stare at me! Say something!

Bibi It's too late.

Louise (*confused*) Too late. What do you mean too late?

Bibi It's too late to do all those things you were talking about.

Louise (*softly*) Why? Why is it too late ...?

Bibi Well, I did something this afternoon too. I didn't just sit around hating myself for being born like I usually do when I'm upset, I did something different.

Louise (*sinking into a chair at the table; staring at her*) What?

Bibi I thought.

Louise (*impressed*) That is different.

Bibi I thought hard about everything I'd read about Jane Goodall's meteoric rise to fame and when I came to the conclusion that I had twisted all of it to suit my ridiculous fantasies about being a scientist, I began to wonder why I'd been carrying on all these years about rushing off on expeditions I'd never go on.

Louise And?

Bibi (*suddenly; ashamed*) I'm not legitimate!

Louise I had no idea! And both of your parents are Catholic.

Bibi I mean who I am isn't legitimate. People don't take me seriously. (*Pause. Softly*) Sometimes, and this is very hard to admit, I get the feeling people think I'm silly.

Louise Never!

Bibi But no-one ever thinks a scientist is silly, do they?

Louise I never have.

Bibi As a scientist, I felt respected. I even thought the men respected me, but they didn't really. Most of them didn't believe I was a scientist and the few who did thought I was a silly scientist. (*She groans*) Oh, and the men, the men. I'm so ashamed. Why do I do that? Why do I let horrible strangers victimize me over and over?

Louise Bad taste.

Bibi No. Fear.

Louise Well, after meeting some of those men, I can understand why you're afraid.

Bibi I'm never afraid of them. They don't know or care about me. What could they do to me? Steal some old kitchen equipment, turn up late for lunch? (*Softly*) I'm only afraid of people who know and love me. When they leave, they leave me. Cowards feel safe loving strangers.

Louise (*suddenly; anxiously*) Bibi! What does all this have to do with being too late?

Bibi (*hesitating, then quickly; upset*) I just realized I had to start living my life as if it was real. I had to start doing things that counted or I wouldn't have a life ... I knew the time had come for me to make my move and if I didn't seize the moment and do it, the moment would never come again, so I did it, Louise. I made my move.

Louise (*alarmed*) What do you mean? What move?

Bibi stares at her, unable to speak

(*Standing up quickly*) Out with it, Bibi. What did you do?
Bibi I took the job in New York!

Louise stares at her, then slowly sinks back down into her chair

Louise (*stricken*) No.
Bibi Yes. I had to. I've spent my whole life failing at things I can't do, Louise. It's time for me to grow up, be brave and start failing at what I can do.
Louise (*softly*) But what will I do without you ...?
Bibi (*lost*) I don't know. What will I do without you? You're the only person who's ever been able to make me laugh just when I'm about to commit suicide ... and when I'm at my dumbest, only you know I'm being incredibly smart.
Louise There won't be anybody to play games with in the evening, and if there is they won't dare tease me about how my hand shakes with excitement just before I win. Everyone else thinks I'm sweet and self-sacrificing ... a sainted mother ... only you ever figured out I was a raging, selfish egotist with a consuming desire to compete and win ... (*Suddenly, hopefully*) The things you said to me, Bibi, they weren't all true, were they?
Bibi (*quietly*) Well ... yes, Louise ... I'm afraid they were ... (*Quickly; reassuringly*) But no matter what he looks like, I'm sure Clark is a wonderful person.

Louise shrugs in dismissal, then a faint, sad smile touches her lips

Louise How can either one of us ever explain to anyone else how we got here? We'll be so alone.
Bibi (*with tears filling her eyes*) I'll be alone, but you don't have to be! David would come back in a minute if you asked him!
Louise (*with a deep sigh*) I couldn't. I'd feel like a cheap coward, devoid of all self-respect, without character, pride or spirit.
Bibi (*dismissively*) Oh, you'd get over that. (*Encouragingly*) A good marriage can survive a small indiscretion, Louise.
Louise Oh, I don't care about his affair. I probably would have done exactly what he did except it's impossible to meet new people in the cellar. (*She sighs*) We used our marriage up, Bibi. Call it mismanagement, I don't know, all I know is I have to find my way alone now. I guess we all do.

They sink into their own sad thoughts for a moment, then Bibi looks at her

Bibi It's funny, isn't it?

Louise What?

Bibi How you make things happen to yourself, even when you don't want them to happen. I mean, just yesterday morning everything was like it always was and now it's all over.

Louise I know. I miss them already, those sweet, lying days when we knew that every day would be like the day before and the day after.

Bibi We were miserable.

Louise I know, but now that it's ending I remember it as a happy time. The good times ahead will never be as a good as all those rotten times with you. The last three horrible years were three of the most wonderful years of my life!

Bibi Mine too! Oh, Louise! Where will I ever find another friend like you?

Louise You won't, but why do you have to? This isn't the end of our friendship, for God's sake. (*She gives a shaky laugh*) We're behaving as if one of us is about to die!

Bibi You're right. We're being ridiculous.

Pause

Louise But it will never be the same between us again, will it?

Bibi No. You have to be there every minute for it to be this way. Once I leave the threads will begin to unravel whether we want them to or not ...

Louise You'll fly in from New York for a visit and we'll catch up ... but you can't catch up on long silences, you can't catch up on going through it together, you can't catch up on everything.

Bibi (*fighting back tears*) And what about dropping by? Dropping by is so important. Think of all those summer nights when I'd come by after work and we'd drink iced tea on the back porch. The sound of the boys playing in the dark garden ... their sweet voices ... the next time I see them they will have grown and I won't be part of their memories. At best, I'll just be a person they tell things to ... (*Frantically*) I don't have to go you know!

Louise (*hopefully*) No, you don't. I mean, making your move doesn't mean you actually have to move physically, does it? It could also mean ... (*She stops, at a loss*)

Bibi (*brightly*) Thinking differently!

Louise (*enthusiastically*) Of course! Thinking differently is very important!

Bibi I can develop a fresh attitude!

Louise Look at life with a new eye!

Bibi Adopt a revolutionary point of view!

Louise (*suddenly flat*) And then what? (*With a lost sigh*) No, Bibi. Thinking isn't enough for people like us. We have to do things and you have to go. (*With forced cheer*) And New York will be great. You're going to be a wild success.

Bibi (*startled*) A success? What an extraordinary thought. I was satisfied with failing at something I can do ... (*Excitedly*) Actually, I do have the touch, you know. Food comes to life in my hands. Oh, Louise, the possibilities are endless! I could end up with my own cookbooks, my own line of kitchen utensils ... you know how I'm always bending and twisting things because they don't work right ... maybe one day I'll be invited to cook a meal in the White House! Influential people will come from all over the world simply to taste my chicken and dumplings! Louise! We're lying again!

Louise No, we're not! This isn't a lie, this is a dream! You can pull it off!

Bibi How can I do anything without you to talk to?

Louise Talk to yourself. That's all I was doing when you walked in. The conversation is part of us now. You know what I'd say and I know what you'd say.

They stare at each other, deeply moved, then Louise suddenly gets up and walks to the dummy, trying to lighten her mood

(*With forced cheer*) Hey, and every cloud has a silver lining, doesn't it? Earlier today, while I was thinking about killing David, I came up with some terrific ideas for the vests. Look at this! (*She picks up some brown pieces of paper, then suddenly stops and looks at Bibi. Anxiously*) The vests, Bibi! Lie or dream?

Bibi Dream!

Louise (*excitedly*) Oh, good, because I was thinking about fish all afternoon for some reason and I had a vision. What do you think of a vest in a fish-scale pattern, all the scales a different colour?

Bibi (*excitedly*) That's brilliant, Louise! (*She pauses. Heartbroken*) But I can't really talk about it right now ...

Louise slowly turns to look at her as Bibi stands up

Louise (*tensely*) Why not ...?

Bibi Well, I was afraid if I waited too long to go to New York I'd lose my nerve.

Louise (*tensely, anxiously*) So?

Bibi So since I have most of the things I care about in those two suitcases ... (*she pauses*) I'm going now, Louise.

Louise Now ...?
Bibi Yeah ... I called a taxi. I said I'd meet him on the road.

They stare at each other for a moment, then Louise rushes over to her and they hold each other for a moment. They step back from each other, both in tears

Bibi Thanks for packing my bags for me.
Louise I didn't just pack them, I finished your laundry too. I can't say goodbye.
Bibi No. Neither can I.
Louise Let's just pretend you're running over to your place to get some fabric softener, OK?
Bibi OK. (*In a forced normal voice*) I've run out of fabric softener, Louise. I'll be right back.
Louise (*in a normal voice*) OK, Bibi. I'll see you in a minute.

They look at each other, then as Bibi picks up her suitcases and starts out the door, Louise grabs her papers and pins and walks to the dummy. Just before Bibi disappears out the door, the phone suddenly rings. Bibi quickly turns back. Louise looks at her, then walks to the phone and picks up the receiver.

Louise Hallo? (*She hesitates, then turns to Bibi and holds out the receiver. Tensely*) It's for you.

Without thinking, Bibi steps forward with excitement, then suddenly stops. She hesitates, then takes a deep breath

Bibi It's too late. I'm gone.
Louise (*into the phone*) Sorry. You just missed her. ... No. I'm afraid she won't be coming back. ... That's right. ... Goodbye. (*She triumphantly replaces the receiver, then turns to look at Bibi*)

They stare at each other for a moment

Bibi (*fighting back tears*) Well, I guess I'd better get that fabric softener.
Louise Yeah ... (*Urgently, emotionally*) Don't take too long!
Bibi (*quietly*) No. I won't take too long. (*Pause. Tenderly*) So long, Mamie.

Louise studies her as if she'd give anything to make her stay

Louise (*quietly*) So long, Mamie.

Bibi quickly turns and walks out the door. As she walks to the steps Louise grabs her pins and papers again, goes to the dummy and starts working frantically to keep herself distracted

As she works, David suddenly appears in Clark's doorway under the stairs wearing a dinner-jacket and drinking champagne

David (*happily*) I'm not saying it was you who held me back, Louise. I couldn't have gotten through those bad years without you ... but ever since our divorce, well, things have been very good for me ...

Louise starts singing to drive the defeating fantasy away as David continues speaking

I'm overwhelmed by major commissions ... (*He gives a quick laugh*) I'm so busy I don't even have time to pick up all the awards I receive ... (*Self-satisfied*) And I'm very happy with my new wife, she's a wonderful person, so bright, so kind ... she's taught me how to let go of my anger, Louise ... it's too bad it couldn't have been that way with us ... but how else do you learn ...?

Louise (*over the above; singing triumphantly*)
>East side, West side,
>All around the town,
>The tots play ring around rosy,
>London Bridge is falling down...

As David finishes speaking he disappears back into the gloom and exits

Bibi pauses just before going up the hillside steps to look back at the house with longing

Louise and Bibi (*singing joyfully*)
>Boys and girls together,
>Me and Mamie O'Rourke,
>We'll trip the light fantastic ...!

Black-out

CURTAIN

FURNITURE AND PROPERTY LIST

ACT I
SCENE 1

On stage: Washing machine
Drier containing clothes
Table
Chairs
Easy chair
Refrigerator. *In it*: milk, eggs, bread, vegetables (including lettuce and carrots)
Kitchen fixtures
Kettle
Tea cups
Pots
Glasses
Alarm clock
Bowl of cornflakes
Coffee machine
Toaster (practical)
Bowl
Egg whisk
Carrot peeler
Sledge-hammer (under the staircase)
Dusting cloth
Broom
Record player (practical)
Dressmaker's dummy with paper vest

Off stage: Two suitcases containing coloured clothes (**Bibi**)
Rubble (**Stage Management**)
Martini (**Clark**)

SCENE 2

Strike: Rubble

Set: **Bibi's** open suitcases, spilling clothes
Bottle of wine (open)
2 half-full glasses of wine
Stack of magazines
Scissors

Off stage: Herbs (**Bibi**)

Personal: **Clark:** stethoscope
Bibi: (apron)

ACT II
SCENE 1

Strike: Bottle of wine
Glasses

Off stage: Rubble (**Stage Management**)

Personal: **Clark:** pilot's helmet, cigarette, fish head mask

SCENE 2

Strike: Rubble
Bibi's suitcases

Set: **Bibi's** suitcases, packed up and shoved into a corner
2 duffle bags
Small circles of brown paper
Pins

Off stage: Sledge hammer (**David**)
Glass of champagne (**David**)

LIGHTING PLOT

Single interior setting with exterior backing
Practical fittings required: table lamps, pendant light

ACT I, SCENE 1

To open: Morning effect

Cue 1   **Louise:** "Rebuild!"   (Page 16)
           Black-out

ACT I, SCENE 2

To open: Spot c on **Clark** and **Louise**

Cue 2   **Clark** holds **Louise** tightly   (Page 17)
           Bring up very slowly to interior (night time) effect; fade
               up practical lamps, fade out spot

Cue 3   **Bibi** and **Louise** turn to the telephone   (Page 29)
           Black-out

ACT II, SCENE 1

To open: Late morning effect

Cue 4   **Clark:** "... I warned you, didn't I?"   (Page 44)
           Black-out

ACT II, SCENE 2

To open: Early evening effect with sunset, intensifying gradually
               throughout the scene. Table lamps and pendant on

Cue 5   **Louise** and **Bibi:** "... the light fantastic ...!"   (Page 59)
           Black-out

EFFECTS PLOT

ACT I

Cue 1   To open   (Page 1)
Washer and drier noises (loud); sound of electric kettle
    starting to boil

Cue 2   **Louise:** "... doesn't mean he can't hear!"   (Page 1)
The washer rocks violently and makes a
    grinding noise; the kettle whistles sharply; the
    alarm clock goes off. Cut effect when Louise turns
    off or kicks the relevant appliance

Cue 3   **David** comes downstairs   (Page 2)
The washer rocks and makes the grinding
    noise (as in Cue 2). Cut effects when David
    kicks the washer

Cue 4   **Bibi:** "That can't be right."   (Page 7)
A ripping sound, then a tremendous crash

Cue 5   **Bibi** walks through the door   (Page 7)
Smoke (for plaster dust effect)

Cue 6   Intermittently throughout pages 7-12   (Page 7)
Faint sound of hammering, occasional
    small crashes

Cue 7   **Louise:** "... maybe I should have ——"   (Page 12)
Noise on the stairs

Cue 8   To open SCENE 2   (Page 16)
Music: a late Beethoven quartet plays softly;
    fade gradually after lights come up to full

Cue 9   **Bibi:** "... mangy piece of ——"   (Page 17)
The telephone rings

Cue 10   **Bibi:** "Unlike Felix."   (Page 18)
The telephone rings

A licence issued by Samuel French Ltd to perform this play does not include permission to use the incidental music specified in this copy. Where the place of performance is already licensed by the Performing Right Society a return of music used must be made to them. If the place of performance is not so licensed then application should be made to the PERFORMING RIGHT SOCIETY, 29 Berners Street, London W1.

A separate and additional licence from PHONOGRAPHIC PERFORMANCES LTD, Ganton House, Ganton Street, London W1, is needed whenever commercial recordings are used.